THE COMPLETE POTTER

PORCELAIN

THE COMPLETE POTTER
PORCELAIN

CAROLINE WHYMAN

SERIES EDITOR: EMMANUEL COOPER

University of Pennsylvania Press
Philadelphia

This book is dedicated to my mother and father and to Kevin, for without their support it could not have been completed. My thanks also go to Pat, for her invaluable advice and criticism (as well as her humour!), and to the potters who contributed their knowledge and photographs.

It is also dedicated to my teachers and to all other teachers and students, in the hope that, by sharing information and experience – however small – we will not have to keep re-inventing the wheel!

Copyright © 1994 by Caroline Whyman

First published 1994 by B.T. Batsford, Ltd.

First published in the United States 1994 by the University of Pennsylvania Press

Library of Congress Cataloguing-in-Publication Data

Whyman, Caroline.
    Porcelain / Caroline Whyman.
      p.   cm. – (The Complete potter)
    Includes bibliographical references and index.
    ISBN 0-8122-3300-X
    1. Pottery craft–Handbooks, manuals, etc. 2. Porcelain–Handbooks, manuals, etc. I. Title. II. Series.
    TT920.W49   1994
    738.1′4–dc20   94-12445
                                              CIP

ISBN-0-8122-3300-X

Front cover: **Caroline Whyman** *Porcelain bowl decorated with underglaze blue, with gold, platinum and colored lusters. Height approx. 35 cm (14 in.). Collection of Mr. A. Bartley, New York*

Back cover: **Elaine Coleman** *Incised porcelain teapot with clear glaze*

Frontispiece: **Caroline Whyman** *Inlaid porcelain dish, diameter 33 cm (13 in)*

Page 6: **Loraine Rutt** *"Lapstrake Vessel." Porcelain with molochite on driftwood base, 18 × 10 × 35 cm (7 × 4 × 14 in). Coiled onto etched porcelain and then assembled. Texture enhanced using oxides and commercial stains on leather-hard clay. Fired to 1260*C (2300*F)*

CONTENTS

PREFACE

Although this book is written in chapters covering various techniques, the pleasure and surprise of creation often lies in the mixing and blending of techniques to realize ideas. Each chapter should therefore be regarded as a guide for experiment, rather than a rule, and it is worth remembering that an apparent disaster sometimes carries the seed of inspiration for a new idea or method.

Porcelain is a vast subject, impossible to cover completely in one book, but I hope that the book will encourage you to try working with porcelain, and to gain the confidence to pursue your own line of enquiry through further investigation.

Stoneware mould for impressing decoration on the interior of Ting-ware bowls, Jin dynasty (AD 1184). 22 cm (8½in) diameter. Courtesy of the Percival David Foundation of Chinese Art

CHAPTER ONE

A BRIEF HISTORY OF PORCELAIN

The name 'china', given to semi-transparent or white-bodied ware, is a direct reference to the origins of porcelain in China, and to the 'China trade' which developed with Europe, where porcelain was regarded as rare, exotic and mysterious. The secret of porcelain took around 200 years to unravel, but research on the subject led to the development of many white bodies, some of which form the basis of production for most of the pottery industry today.

CHINA

The birth of porcelain in China was not a sudden event. It was more of an organic process of refinement and development, reliant on an abundance of appropriate materials and the advanced technical skills of pottery making, set within the environment of a very sophisticated culture. The original use of the term 'porcelain' in Chinese was applied to pots which made a distinct ringing sound when struck, and not to the qualities of whiteness and translucence which predominate now. This 'porcelain', in association with food, was therefore capable of delighting all five senses.

More than 3,000 years ago, Chinese potters were using down-draught kilns to high-fire a smooth white clay to 1200°C (2192°F), and, by the third century AD, the pale greeny-blue Yue ware closely resembled porcelain. These early pots were skilfully made in press moulds and on the wheel, but were rather rigidly shaped in imitation of the bronze and jade vessels of the time.

Kiln firing improved with the development of multi-chambered hill kilns, in which the lowest chambers reached even higher stoneware temperatures.

THE T'ANG DYNASTY

During the T'ang dynasty (AD 618–906), saggars were used to protect the ware from ash and smoke, and the 'bag wall' was added to the kiln to direct and deflect the flame. Trade outside China in this early porcelain was established to the Middle East and, by sea, to Japan, and very small amounts survived the precarious overland journey to Europe. At this time, persistent efforts were made in China to create a fine white body, not only for court use but also for funerary purposes, as white was the colour associated with death and mourning.

THE SONG DYNASTY

During the 300-odd years of the Song dynasty (AD 960–1279), some of the most beautiful pots of all were made; with their quiet, restrained forms and sumptuous glazes they are considered by many to represent the quintessential achievement of the Chinese potters.

The north of China was known at this time for a beautiful and delicate porcelain known as Ting ware. This finely thrown and turned creamy body has recently been discovered to be 'a clay-rich, lime-fluxed type not unlike early Meissen', which may account for its tendency to warp. The Ting potters devised special saggars to overcome the warping, in which the bowls were fired on their rims. The saggars were ingeniously designed so that a series of graduated bowls could be fired on top of each other in a single saggar, separated on internal steps which could accommodate many more pieces than in a conventional saggar. Typically, bowls and dishes were decorated with crisp but fluid carvings of flowers and birds, and were glazed with a thinly applied, faintly ivory glaze which flowed into the detail. The unglazed rims were finished by adding a precisely made band of copper alloy.

A later innovation of the Ting potters was the use of hump moulds made from smooth, high-fired stoneware and carved with complex designs. These moulds could be used by less-skilled workers to repeat work with raised patterns, but they lacked the fluid, spontaneous quality of the earlier hand-carved Ting bowls, which were prized by the Imperial Court.

In the twelfth century, towards the latter half of the Song dynasty, the Imperial Court moved south, and this, coupled with the increase in trade, gave impetus to the southern potteries. This stimulated the

Whiteware vase, Song Dynasty (early twelfth century). Porcelain with blue-toned Quing Bai-type glaze, height 18 cm (7 in). Courtesy of the Percival David Foundation of Chinese Art

development and production of large quantities of celadons – beautiful pale green or grey-blue glazes covering a porcelain body which was often carved. (Northern celadons were often a darker olive-green in colour.) Some of the celadons had bodies that were almost white, and sometimes faintly translucent. These are often referred to as 'porcelanous', which is misleading, but indicates a gradual progression towards a true, white, translucent porcelain.

During the Song dynasty, abundant raw materials were found around Ch'ing-te Chen in southern China. A porcelain industry consequently developed in that area, supported by a skilled and diverse labour force, to supply the increasing demand for porcelain. Estimates by Chinese archaeologists suggest that a single Ch'ing-te Chen kiln was capable of holding 20–25,000 pots in each firing, which is an indication of the scale and importance of these potteries. The kilns were sophisticated, with spy holes and stoke holes in each chamber so that the temperature and atmosphere could be carefully controlled.

The extremely sensuous quality of some of the glazes, applied to simple forms, reached a pinnacle in the rare Kuan pieces made for the Imperial Court. Their crackled glazes were likened to jade, the finest being a pale grey-blue.

Ch'ing-Pai porcelain was sometimes compared to the northern Ting ware. This was also made over hump moulds and carved, but the glaze and the formal patterns of flowers in panels, with dotted comb-marks to fill the spaces, lacked the quality of the best Ting pots.

THE YUAN DYNASTY

During the short period of the Yuan dynasty (AD 1280–1367), a pale, blueish-green porcelain ware called Shu-fu was made near Ch'ing-te Chen. Often decorated in low relief with flowers and phoenixes, and coloured with copper and cobalt, this was the forerunner of the techniques and glazes which would characterize the Ming pots of the next dynasty (AD 1368–1644).

By the fourteenth century, Ch'ing-te Chen was one of the most populous cities on earth, supplying a good part of the known world with both everyday and 'prestige' porcelain. At this time there was an increased demand for fine-quality ware, initially from the Middle East and the Philippines, and eventually from the rest of the developed world. This tremendous production was maintained by a labour force which was efficiently divided to perform specific tasks. The potteries were also supported by good river transport.

THE MING DYNASTY

Following the change from the Yuan to the Ming dynasty, a new style of porcelain was developed. This used underglaze painting with cobalt, and produced the characteristic 'blue and white' of Ming porcelain. The local cobalt was very impure and fired to a grey-blue; it was only during the fourteenth century that a relatively pure form of cobalt was traded to China from Persia. By mixing these two cobalts, a distinctive and beautiful blue was made. The indigenous skills of the Chinese people, whose written language was formed with a brush, must have greatly facilitated the increasingly complex and fine painting of the underglaze blue decoration.

Enamelling – the process of painting bright, low-temperature colours over the glazed porcelain – was developed in the middle of the fifteenth century. This enabled the colours of yellow, purple, bright green and red to elaborate the underglaze-blue designs, often with little regard for naturalistic colour because of the limited palette. It would be another 150 years before the enamel palette was extended to include a wide range of greens known as *famille vert*, which allowed the decoration to become more imaginative and skilful.

The Dutch East India Company, founded in 1602, formed direct trading routes between Europe and the Far East, and therefore played a major role in the enormous increase in production of Chinese porcelain. As the demand for porcelain in Europe grew, the forms and decoration of the exported porcelain changed to reflect a more 'European' taste, but there was still a large market for Chinese forms and decoration within China. These pots were beautifully and naturalistically painted with themes of flowers, fruit, birds and rocks, which were very carefully composed so that their greater philosophical and symbolic meanings – universally understood by the Chinese – were harmonious and balanced. They were a reflection of 'the Great Tao', and a reminder of the unity of all things – not only the universe, nature and man, but also in daily life. (Phillip Rawson and Laszlo Legeza's book, *Tao, The Chinese Philosophy of Time and Change* [see the Bibliography on page 109], contains many fascinating references to the meanings and symbols in Chinese art.)

By the end of the Ming period, the qualities of oriental porcelain were widely known in Europe. Early European attempts to make the blue-and-white porcelain influenced the development of Delft and Majolica, but these were low-fired bodies which had to be biscuited (many Chinese pots were single-fired) before being glazed and decorated. Sometimes, after the cobalt was painted on the tin glaze, a second, transparent glaze was applied on top, in an attempt to imitate the qualities of Chinese porcelain.

THE CH'ING DYNASTY

During the last great dynasty of China, known as Ch'ing (1644–1912), the Imperial porcelain factory was rebuilt. The forms and decoration that it produced, although technically perfect, were rather cool, hard and clinical in feeling. Eventually, even the 'meaning' inherent in the earlier decoration was lost. In part, this may have been

Blanc-de-Chine statue of Guan Yin, seventeenth century. Height 26.2 cm (10¼in). Courtesy of the Percival David Foundation of Chinese Art

attributable to the European demand for a combination of oriental and Western themes in the decoration, and for Western items such as dinner, tea, and cruet sets, which were exported by the million.

New techniques in the Ch'ing period increased the colour range of transparent and opaque enamels. The stability of the colours also allowed them to be shaded and painted without bleeding into each other. *Famille rose* enamel, which uses gold to make delicate pink enamels, originated in France, but was perfected in China and used to paint flora and fauna on porcelain in minute detail.

Monochrome glazes also became popular, and were applied on simple forms, their bright colours enhanced by the white porcelain body. Typical colours were a vivid lemon yellow, transparent alkaline turquoise, rose pink and a pale green which was 'compounded and opacified by the mortally dangerous arsenical oxide' (Margaret Medley, *The Chinese Potter* [see the Bibliography on page 109]). Possibly the best-known glaze, however, was 'peach bloom', which still remains elusive and difficult to achieve. A transparent with varying additions of copper, the peach bloom glaze was gently reduced to give a delicate and often speckled range of colour, from pink through to a mossy green. On some pots, two glazes were used: for example, 'Robin's egg' glaze, in which a dark blue glaze was sprayed over an opaque turquoise glaze.

There were other provincial centres for making porcelain, as well as the area of Ch'ing-te Chen. Swatow, in northern China, exported porcelain to South-East Asia, Indonesia and Japan for about a hundred years. Swatow ware was cheerfully decorated with enamels in red, green and bright turquoise, with some black outlines beneath, but the quality of the clay and the standard of the work was variable.

Fukien province became known for making *blanc-de-Chine* (see photograph). This body was extremely smooth, white and glassy, with a brilliant, thinly applied transparent glaze. On the best examples, this glaze became so completely integrated with the body that it appeared to be made from a single material. *Blanc-de-Chine* was generally used to model figures of deities; Guan Yin, the Buddhist goddess of mercy, was a popular subject. The modelling was extremely skilful, the robes and figures having a sinuous, curvilinear quality that emphasized the smooth, plastic quality of the porcelain. The overall effect was one of sensuous perfection, and awe at the technical virtuosity of the makers.

JAPAN AND KOREA

EARLY PORCELAIN
Porcelain was produced in Korea as early as the tenth century. It reflected the influence of the Song potters in style and technique, but the best of these Korean pots have a more vigorous and less formal approach to

decoration, with very lively and spontaneous brushwork. These qualities were certainly admired by the Japanese, and it was a Korean potter, Ri Senpei, forcibly brought to Japan with other potters after the invasion of Korea, who discovered in AD 1600 that the mountain of Izumiyama, in southern Japan, was composed of a fine porcelain stone. This area, known as Arita, and the nearby port of Imari, are still strongly linked with the manufacture and export of Japanese porcelain, and Izumiyama is now a large quarry pit. Its finest porcelain stone is exhausted, although new deposits of quality porcelain stone have been found nearby.

Initially, the imported Ming porcelains influenced the Japanese potters. The famous Arita potter, Kakiemon, perfected the technique of onglaze enamel and underglaze blue in the Chinese style, but subsequent Japanese potters developed a style that was recognizably their own. This would be copied by the British porcelain factories at Derby and Worcester during the eighteenth century. Within Japan, regional styles developed, such as the bold Kutani ware, noted for its combination of purple, yellow, blue, vivid green and red enamels with underglaze blue, often with an onglaze black outline painted beneath the colourful enamels.

THE EIGHTEENTH CENTURY
During the eighteenth century, an enormous amount of Japanese porcelain was made for export, its production being increased by the development of transfer techniques for duplicating decoration. Unlike the photo-silkscreen techniques used today to make technically identical patterns, the Japanese method used tissue paper painted with powdered charcoal to transfer the *outline* of the design to the pot. This was then skilfully hand-painted either on to the biscuited pot in underglaze blue, or on to the glazed pot with enamel.

THE TWENTIETH CENTURY
The eighteenth-century technique using charcoal and tissue paper for transferring designs is still used today in Japan by potters who are neither totally industrialized nor working as 'individual' studio potters, as in the West. They usually comprise small groups of skilled craftspeople, often headed by a painter or decorator whose 'name' is given to the work. Although one-off pieces may be hand-decorated by the 'named' head of the pottery, a cheaper ware is produced by slip-casting, with the master's design transferred to the pot and then hand-painted by skilled decorators. This semi-industrial porcelain forms part of a very gradual and integrated line between 'industrial' and 'studio' ceramics which continues in Japan to this day.

This technique of transferring designs to pots using powdered charcoal and tissue paper is also used by a contemporary British potter, Russell Coates (see pages 44–7).

EUROPE

THE SEVENTEENTH CENTURY
By the seventeenth century, the qualities of porcelain were known in Europe and, although many attempts were made to emulate it, few were successful. John Dwight make a type of salt-glazed porcelain, but it never became a commercial success. It was not until 1709 that Bottger, a German chemist, devised a formula for porcelain, which became the foundation for production of porcelain at the Meissen factory a year later.

Many other attempts were made to formulate a porcelain body, based on a combination of documentary evidence and geological and chemical knowledge, as well as guesswork and industrial espionage! White firing bodies were devised, and some were even translucent; the most successful ones closely matched oriental porcelain or became new bodies in their own right. Many of these bodies proved too difficult to work commercially, however, and were only used for short periods of time. An early French attempt made from a glassy frit mixed with clay gave a porcelain-like body known as 'soft paste' because it matured at a low temperature, but it distorted easily unless the temperature was finely controlled, and many losses resulted. The first soft paste in England was developed and used in Chelsea.

THE EIGHTEENTH CENTURY

European porcelain remained difficult to make and fire for most of the eighteenth century. It was costly to manufacture and was unable to compete with (literally) millions of imported pieces from the Orient, and so became a luxury product for rich patrons. By the end of the century, however, several discoveries had changed this emphasis dramatically.

The introduction in 1740 of moulds made of plaster of Paris, credited to Ralph Davis, quickly superseded the press moulds of the day, enabling the speedy repetition of pots 'in the round' by a less skilled workforce. Research continued to improve their resistance to warping, and the discovery of China clay deposits at Limoges, in France, led to the development of high-fired or 'hard-paste' porcelain which was less prone to warping. Similar bodies were made in England, the most noteworthy at the Worcester pottery. Another research development was Parian porcelain, a creamy, mid-temperature body made from a mixture of China clay and feldspar. Initially, Parian porcelain was used for figurines (and, later, for some vessels) and, left unglazed, had a smooth, marble-like quality which enhanced the modelling of fine detail.

THE NINETEENTH CENTURY

Large deposits of China clay were also found in Cornwall, in south-west England, as well as 'Cornish stone', which formed the basis for hard-paste porcelain. But it was the addition of 50 per cent bone ash (calcined bones) to the recipe, perfected by Josiah Spode, which produced a body known as 'bone china', and this propelled the expansion of the pottery industry into the Industrial Revolution of the nineteenth century. Bone china proved to be an extremely translucent, white body, less prone to warping than previous bodies. It was biscuited at a high temperature, but glazed at a *lower* temperature, therefore giving a less durable glaze. It was also termed 'soft paste'.

The popular enamel decoration of the early European porcelains reflected oriental inspiration, but, as the impetus of the Industrial Revolution grew, European styles evolved, particularly in Germany and France. Porcelain factories were established in Paris, Vienna, Berlin, Dresden, Meissen, Sevres and Copenhagen. In England, the potteries in Staffordshire, Worcester and Derby supplied a worldwide demand for tableware and ornamental ceramics, figurines, commemorative busts and a wide range of souvenirs.

Towards the end of the nineteenth century, the development of the essentially European style of Art Nouveau, based on the sinuous and natural qualities of plant forms, was particularly suited to the medium of porcelain, and many exotic glazes were developed to complement the sensuous forms. At this time, the ideas and philosophy of William Morris and John Ruskin re-evaluated the qualities of 'hand-made' artefacts, and became the seed for the revival of these crafts during the next century.

THE TWENTIETH CENTURY

During the first half of the twentieth century, the porcelain manufacturers of Europe endured two world wars, when they either

David Leach *Thrown and carved porcelain teapot. Height 23 cm (9 in)*

ceased production or were mostly limited to making tableware. A few factories employed artists, potters and designers to work in special studios within the factories, but the general trend was towards the manufacture of earthenware and stoneware rather than porcelain. There were exceptions, including Emile Dacoeur, who experimented with a porcelain body in France, and the excellent milky-white bodies used for figurines made at the Royal Copenhagen pottery in Denmark. Links between artists and industry were less common in Britain, although in the 1930s a connection was formed between Bullers (manufacturers of industrial porcelain insulators) and the students of Burslem School of Art, who experimented with the porcelain body.

Much of the credit for the revival of studio pottery in Britain, and, to an extent, in the USA, is due to the work of Bernard Leach, a potter, writer, teacher and philosopher. His interest in porcelain was secondary to his achievements in stoneware, but he did make a porcelain body in 1950, although this was not very translucent. It was the research undertaken by his son, David Leach, with the help of Edward Burke, which resulted in the development of a highly plastic porcelain

body with good translucence. This body was eventually available commercially and, through the publication of the recipe, became a point of reference for new porcelain bodies. David Leach's work in porcelain is noted for his finely thrown and fluted bowls and teapots, and decorated vases.

During the 1960s, interest in the orientally

Lucie Rie Porcelain pot. White with inlaid lines, dark brown interior, height 17.2 cm (6¾in), 1966. Courtesy of Ceramic Review

inspired stonewares of Leach and his followers waned, and the work of Lucie Rie gradually gained a new audience with a more contemporary concern for 'modern design'. Her elegant and meticulously formed porcelain and stoneware pots, with their minimal decoration of finely scratched and inlaid lines, and her mastery of unusual and colourful glazes, marked her as one of the twentieth century's greatest potters, and increased the interest in porcelain among potters and the public. As the use of porcelain gained momentum, the hand-built pots based on natural forms by Ruth Duckworth, who had moved to the USA, and the delicate pinched forms of Mary Rogers, working in England, pushed the material to new limits. Eileen Nisbet, whose inspiration lay in fine art rather than the vessel, used porcelain made of very thin slabs for translucent sculptures which she assembled after the slabs were fired and decorated.

The use of porcelain has increased dramatically in the countries in which crafts have been fostered and recognized, and there have been many developments in technique and style. An enormous amount of information has been shared between potters and artists, in publications and workshops, and increasingly through the medium of video and television. The new limits of porcelain lie less in technical skill, which can be honed and improved, or in the limits of the material, than in the scope and imagination of the artists.

CHAPTER TWO

PORCELAIN – THE RAW MATERIAL

Porcelain is not easy to define, as there is no exact point at which white porcelaneous stoneware ends and porcelain begins. Both of these clays are high-fired, vitrified, white bodies. In comparison to white stoneware, however, porcelain is usually more completely vitrified, a truer white in colour, and, where it is thinly formed, has the special quality of translucence. Porcelain has a finer texture than white stoneware, so that, even when left unglazed, it has a satiny-smooth surface that is complete in itself.

Semi-porcelain, or proto-porcelain, as the name suggests, is not regarded by all potters as true porcelain. The increased amounts of ball clay and bentonite in semi-porcelain make it easier to handle and throw, but it is often darker in colour than true porcelain and is rarely translucent.

Left: **Delan Cookson** *Thrown forms, altered by cutting and joining leather-hard pots to create strong, sharp forms*

READY-MADE PORCELAINS

As recently as thirty years ago, potters who wished to use porcelain had very little choice but to mix their own, as the porcelains made for industry were designed to be used with the moulded processes. Today, however, there is a wide variety of prepared porcelains for studio use, covering a range of maturing temperatures, qualities and price. Generally, the cheaper bodies are darker and less inclined to be translucent. The whiter bodies contain more refined ingredients, and greater measures are taken to prevent contamination during the processing; they are more expensive as a result.

Knowing the essential qualities that you require from porcelain will help in your choice of body. If you wish to work with colourful opaque glazes, for example, a translucent body is not essential, nor is it important to have the whitest body available;

but if you intend to use a transparent glaze or underglaze painting, the 'whiteness' or 'blueness' of the fired body will be paramount.

Clay manufacturers will give general guidelines as to the qualities of their porcelains, but ask for samples and make some comparative tests before ordering larger quantities. Make a note of the fired results and the working properties of each body (see page 21).

THE COMPOSITION OF PORCELAIN

Unlike many stoneware and earthenware clays, which are frequently composed of naturally occurring secondary-clay deposits, porcelain is an industrially made material. It resembles clay, and is made from white stones and other white material – usually a combination of China clay, feldspar and quartz, with varying additions of ball clay and bentonite, which improve plasticity, especially in throwing bodies. The following recipe, from Daniel Rhodes's book *Stoneware and Porcelain* (see the Bibliography on page 109), is a theoretical starting point for formulating a high-fired (1300°C [2372°F]) porcelain body with good working properties.

Daniel Rhodes: porcelain body

China clay	40
Ball clay	10
Quartz	25
Feldspar	25

Each material has a role to play in the formulation of porcelain, so it is helpful to know about the individual ingredients, as even small alterations to the quantity or the materials will affect the handling qualities, the maturing temperature and the fired results of the porcelain.

CHINA CLAYS (KAOLIN)

These are primary clays, found and mined where they are formed, and are the result of the decomposition of granitic rock through heat and pressure. Due to their large particle size, China clays are not at all plastic (although some China clays are more plastic than others). They form as much as 50 per cent of a porcelain body, and are used for their whiteness, low shrinkage and refactoriness (ability to withstand high temperatures without melting).

China clays contain tiny but variable amounts of titanium and iron, which affect the fired colour of the porcelain; a China clay with the lowest quantity of these impurities will fire the whitest. Analyses of raw materials are generally available from suppliers. Among the whitest firing are 'grolleg', and 'standard porcelain China clay', from English China Clays (see the List of Suppliers on pages 110–11), and 'Edgar' plastic kaolin from the USA (see also pages 110–11), which is slightly creamier. 'Super-standard porcelain China clay', also from English China Clays, is extremely plastic and white, but this increase in quality and refinement is reflected in a higher cost and can make porcelain bodies too sticky.

David Leach: porcelain body

Standard porcelain China clay (English China Clays)	55
FFF potash feldspar (water-ground)	25
Quartz (200-mesh; see below)	15
Bentonite (English China Clays)	3

BALL CLAYS

These are secondary clays, carried from their original source by weathering and erosion, which eventually settle, forming 'secondary' clay deposits. Ball clays are fairly refactory in nature, but, unlike China clays, they have a very fine particle size, making them extremely plastic with a high shrinkage rate. They contain more titanium and iron than China clays, and these have a marked effect on porcelain, making it creamier in oxidation firing and greyer in reduction.

Porcelain bodies can be made without ball clay, but if they contain up to about 10 per cent it greatly improves plasticity and workability, and increases both the dry strength and biscuit strength after firing. The amount of ball clay in porcelain bodies has to be finely balanced between aiding plasticity and strength, and the disadvantages of shrinkage and discoloration.

QUARTZ AND FLINT

These are almost pure silica. Flint, which can be substituted for quartz, is more finely ground but is often less pure. Quartz is supplied in various grades, referred to as 'mesh sizes' – the higher the mesh number, the smaller the particle size. As the maturing temperature and vitrification of porcelain are dependent on the close proximity and intergration of the different particles, it is preferable to use a finely ground quartz of 300-mesh or more. A coarser quartz will increase the maturing temperature of porcelain, or will require a prolonged soak.

In porcelain bodies, quartz is used to increase hardness and strength, and acts as a 'glass former', so the quality of the quartz will affect the translucency. Quartz is added to porcelain bodies in amounts of 15–25 per cent. Too little quartz can result in poor glaze fit, leading to problems of crazing, while too much may cause the porcelain to shatter or crack.

FELDSPARS

Potash feldspar is most commonly used for making porcelain bodies, and many different qualities are available, particularly from the USA. To test feldspars for the whitest and smoothest glassy melt, fire a small mound of different powdered feldspars on a biscuited tile to the desired temperature for porcelain to mature. The amount of potash feldspar will affect the maturing temperature and translucence of the porcelain. The quantity needed is usually about 25 per cent for a body maturing between 1250–1280°C (2282–2336°F), although some porcelains contain as little as 18 per cent or as much as 27 per cent feldspar.

Feldspar is a flux, and large amounts increase translucency but also the tendency to warp and slump. Decreasing the feldspar raises the maturing temperature, and reduces translucence.

Chris Staley: porcelain body (Cones 9–10)

English China clay	55
Custer feldspar	20
Flint	13
Pyrax	12
Avery kaolin	10
Bentonite	3
Molochite, 100-mesh	6

Note: Nepheline syenite, another feldspathic material, can be substituted for part of the feldspar in the recipe, significantly reducing the maturing temperature. Five per cent of nepheline syenite can reduce the maturing temperature by up to two cones, say from Cones 10–11 to 8 or 9.

BENTONITE AND MACALLOID

Bentonite is a secondary clay of extremely fine particle size, with the ability to form colloidal gels, making it exceptionally plastic. Added to porcelain, in small amounts of between 0.5 and 5 per cent, bentonite will greatly improve the plasticity of porcelain. About 2–3 per cent is normal, as larger amounts can cause warping because of its high shrinkage rate. Most bentonites fire to a creamy-buff colour, due to impurities. White-firing bentonites (e.g. Westone–H, a sodium-activated white Texas bentonite) are available (see the List of Suppliers on pages 110–11) and, although more expensive, are advantageous for making porcelain.

Bentonite (and macalloid) is difficult to mix into bodies and glazes because it swells enormously and quickly forms a sticky, lumpy gel. Soaking it overnight in twice its volume of water, and then thoroughly mixing or sieving it, will make it easier to add to other ingredients. Alternatively, simply soak all the ingredients, including the bentonite, for twenty-four hours.

Macalloid behaves in a similar way to bentonite by aiding plasticity, and is therefore valuable in bodies and as a suspension agent in glazes. Macalloid fires whiter than most bentonites, however, and develops plasticity more quickly when added to bodies. Dorothy Feibleman adds 1 per cent macalloid, rather than bentonite, to her coloured porcelain bodies, and finds that they do not need to 'age' before use. However, Angela Fina in her article on 'Improving Plasticity' (*Ceramics Monthly*, Jan. 1984) says of plasticizers such as macalloid, 'the manufacturers warn that they (gradually) break down in the presence of moulds and bacteria. This suggests that bentonite may be more useful, especially if you age your clay.'

MIXING YOUR OWN BODY

It takes time to mix and test porcelain from raw materials, but there are advantages to mixing your own bodies. You can mix small amounts, which are comparatively expensive to buy ready-made; you can select your materials for quality and cost; and you can develop and adapt your own body for specific needs (e.g. to fire to a lower temperature or to reduce shrinkage in large pieces). Additionally, you can make a considerable saving on transport costs if you are located a long distance from the suppliers, as you also pay to transport the water in ready-made porcelain, which can account for an extra 25 per cent of the weight.

Mixing your own porcelain body can be a straightforward process. The methods that you use will depend on the equipment that you have, and the quantity that you wish to

mix. The following guidelines will help you to overcome some of the difficulties of mixing porcelain.

CLEANLINESS AND DUST

The mixing area and all your equipment must be clean and free from metal contamination, which is often caused by flakes of rust from containers or tools and from metal-oxide residues in sieves. Wherever possible, use plastic containers for storage and keep a separate sieve for making white bodies and transparent glazes.

The main problem when handling the dry ingredients for porcelain is the creation of dust, which is a recognized health hazard and can cause irreversible damage to the lungs. This is especially so with quartz and flint, being pure silica, and with the fine-particled clays used to make porcelain. For this reason, you must wear a suitable dust-mask (these are available from pottery suppliers; see pages 110–11) and take great care to avoid agitating the dry materials more than is absolutely necessary. Some potters mix their dry ingredients first, before adding water, but, unless you use dust-extraction equipment or you can mix the ingredients in an enclosed container, this method is not recommended.

Left: **Jack Doherty** *Oval porcelain bowl with inlaid coloured porcelain. Height 23 cm (9 in). Photograph by Sam Hughes*

RECORD-KEEPING AND WEIGHING

There is no substitute for accurate record-keeping, especially during development work. It will enable you to make comparisons, and to record a full description of the ingredients used. A serialized system of numbers and letters relating to each recipe saves noting all this information on the test piece: for example, you could prefix a number for a porcelain body with the letters PB, and a glaze with the letter G, and so on.

It is easy to make a mistake when weighing ingredients, but especially infuriating when the result is beautiful but unrepeatable! Although it may seem an obvious point to make, marking each ingredient off as you weigh it will help to guard against mistakes, especially when you have interruptions during the weighing process.

EQUIPMENT AND METHOD

For mixing small amounts of porcelain, of up to about 25 kg (55 lb), you will need a good pair of scales, two large plastic bins and a clean 200-mesh sieve. (It is much easier to sieve the mixture through a range of sieves from 60- to 200-mesh. If you have an electric mixer and motorized sieve, these will speed the process even more.)

Half-fill one of the bins with water and add the materials in a specific order, from the lightest to the heaviest: the clays, followed by the feldspar, and finally the flint or quartz (follow the instructions for bentonite on page 19). Allow the materials to soak thoroughly until the air has stopped bubbling to the surface (or, better still, overnight). Then mix the materials, preferably with an electric mixer, and sieve them into the second bin.

Leave the resulting slip to settle, and pour or siphon off any excess water. The porcelain slip can then be dried on a plaster batt or in thick biscuit moulds. Covering the batt or mould with a clean cloth will facilitate the removal of the clay.

The ideal way to make large batches of porcelain is to ball mill the ingredients thoroughly, or at least to blunge them (i.e. mix them with water using a machine with revolving paddles), in order to integrate the particles fully. The value of the milling and blunging is to render the particles as small as possible, bringing them into closer contact with each other and surrounding each particle with a thin film of water. This not only increases the plasticity of the body, but can also lower the temperature at which the porcelain matures. The porcelain slip can then be de-watered using a filter press to squeeze out the excess water. This leaves a flat cake of clay which, if it is not too sticky, is finally prepared by processing it through a de-airing pug mill, which has an effect equivalent to two months' 'ageing'.

You can also mix large amounts of porcelain using a dough mixer, with less water than is used for ball milling or blunging. The porcelain must be stored and 'aged' for longer, to allow complete wetting of the particles for optimum plasticity.

STORING, AGEING AND SOURING

Once you have made the porcelain, it will improve noticeably if you allow it to 'age' and 'sour' in a cool but frost-free area. It should be in a softer, wetter condition than you wish to use it, and sealed in plastic bags or bins. The length of storage time will depend not only on the ingredients but also on the storage conditions, and opinions on this vary from two months to several years! Check the porcelain from time to time for increased plasticity and workability.

Ageing is a physical process in which the water in the clay fully wets and coats all the particles, allowing them to slide over each other more easily. The wetted particles also undergo compression, creating suction. Both actions improve the working qualities of the porcelain by increasing plasticity.

Souring, which takes place alongside ageing, is a natural process. Bacteria present in the clay multiply and break down, releasing amino acids, which change the pH of the water content in the clay from an alkaline to a more acidic state. This has a progressively flocculating effect on the clay particles, creating a strong attraction between them and forming a 'gel'.

Ideally, when souring is complete, the resulting clay is strong in use and able to hold its shape. In a young clay, before souring is complete and the relative acidity is low, only the larger particles (mostly kaolin) are flocculated. This porcelain will feel rather stodgy and resistant to pressure, and adding water will make it sticky rather than increasing plasticity. As the acidity increases, the smaller colloidal particles (bentonites) are flocculated and the bonds between the larger clay particles are lost; the porcelain then becomes springy, plastic and responsive, and will stand well. It may also smell (hence the name 'souring') and appear greyer in colour on the inside.

Eileen Lewenstein *Pierced porcelain pots, squashed and altered while forms were still soft. Height 15 and 18 cm (6 and 7 in)*

Soured clay is valuable for the vigorous action of pulling handles, and small amounts speed the growth of bacteria when it is added to new batches of porcelain.

A WORD ABOUT WATER

The slightly acidic pH required for the optimum plasticity of porcelain can be difficult to achieve, as feldspars and bentonites are alkaline in nature, China clays may contain deflocculants (alkaline) from the mining process, and the water supply may be alkaline. Substituting rainwater can improve the results, as will small additions of vinegar. I add just a scant level teaspoon (5 ml) of vinegar to 25 kg (55 lb) of porcelain to improve plasticity, as too much vinegar makes porcelain a short and thirsty clay.

Angela Fina comments in her article entitled 'Porcelain Plasticity Update' (*Ceramics Monthly*, June–Aug. 1985): 'When [over-] vinegared clay ages, [it] becomes alkaline and deflocculates ... Frank [Tucker] researched flocculants and found Epsom salts to be more satisfactory (142 g [5 oz] to 45 kg [100 lb] dry clay) ... Epsom salts will not lower the pH as much as vinegar, but a pH of 7 (i.e. neutral) with Epsom salts feels comparable to a pH of 5.8 with vinegar, as to the plasticity and strength of the clay.' The only problem encountered with this method was occasional edge blistering, which was countered by sanding the bisqued pots.

ASSESSING PORCELAIN

WORKABILITY AND PLASTICITY

Porcelain bodies vary considerably in their qualities of workability and plasticity, but there are two quick methods which will help you to make comparisons between different bodies. For the first method, take a small lump of clay about the size of a large grape, and gently pinch it to form a flat, even sheet. Observe any undue cracking or drying, which may indicate that the body is short, and look for stickiness or flabbiness, as this may mean that the clay needs to be aged more, or the pH adjusted.

Another method, known as the 'knot test', quickly detects the plasticity (or lack of it) of porcelain. Quickly roll out a thin coil of clay to the approximate thickness of a pencil, and then tie it in a simple knot (see photograph). Some porcelains will form tight, perfectly smooth knots, and others will crack.

WARPING AND SHRINKING

Roll out tiles of porcelain about 12 cm (5 in) long and 4 cm (1.5 in) wide to test for warping and shrinking. By making a 10 cm (4 in) line on the plastic clay, you can make checks on the shrinkage and compare it at every stage, from plastic, leather-hard, dry and biscuit to glaze. Observe and record how much or how little each tile has warped in the process, but take care that all the samples are rolled with clay of the same consistency and thickness, and that they are dried out slowly in the

The knot test. *Coiled and knotted porcelain, showing the different working qualities of porcelain bodies. Some are stained with vegetable dye for easy recognition by the manufacturer*

same conditions, in order to make a useful comparison.

In tests carried out on bodies available in the UK, the overall shrinkage from plastic to fired porcelain varied from 12–14.5 per cent at 1250°C (2282°F), and the variation may well be greater in higher firings.

WHITENESS OR COLOUR

Assess the colour of different porcelains by glaze firing several samples with transparent glaze, which makes it easier to define and compare the colours. Choosing a porcelain for its colour will be governed by the type of firing you use, and is ultimately a personal, aesthetic choice. Porcelain fired in oxidation generally results in a warmer, creamier colour range, due to small quantities of iron oxide, and in reduction tends to produce cooler, greyer results. Whatever kind of firing is used, however, some bodies are whiter and have more 'life' than others, which may simply appear dull and dead.

TRANSLUCENCE

You can use samples of porcelain that you pinched to test plasticity to test translucence as well, by firing them with a transparent glaze. By using a thicker tile and pinching out the end, you will see the relationship between translucence and the thickness of the clay more clearly. Some porcelains are only translucent when they are extremely thin. By holding a fired piece close to a light, you should be able to see your fingers outlined as

shadows. You can enhance translucence by soaking the porcelain when it reaches temperature, or by raising the maturing temperature slightly. Both of these procedures are difficult, however, because, the longer the porcelain is soaked or the temperature raised, the nearer the body will be to the point of melting and collapse.

STRENGTH

Fired porcelain is surprisingly strong, but, when it is unfired, or biscuit-fired, it has very little strength compared to other clays. At both these stages, porcelain needs handling with a degree of caution and sensitivity. You can break some of your test tiles when they are unfired, and after biscuit firing, to understand the fragility of porcelain, but this test is not a substitute for the actual experience gained by working with this material.

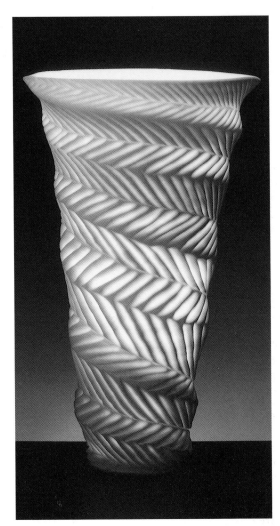

Margaret O'Rorke *Translucent porcelain light, thrown, squashed and then carved. Height 35 cm (13¾in).* Photograph by Chris Honeywell

CHAPTER THREE

THROWING AND TURNING

Centering is a quieting of motion without loss of vitality. It is a vibrant containment. Dynamic centering is never accomplished through sheer will and force. If we are off center, we virtually feel lopsided and excentric; we cannot work unless the clay in finding its center, centers us.

Kenneth R. Beittel, *Zen and the Art of Pottery*

Nearly everyone who has thrown porcelain has a strong opinion about it. Some find porcelain sensuous and exacting, and enjoy coaxing it into shape; others find it exasperating when it suddenly collapses. Porcelain can be soapy, gelatinous and difficult to form into extreme shapes, with abrupt changes in direction – it is less responsive and weaker than a good stoneware, which can be vigorously and directly tackled.

The throwing qualities of porcelain bodies are extremely variable, so try as many as you can and work them beyond their limits to find the one most suitable for you. Some bodies simply will not tolerate being thrown much higher than 20 cm (8 in), but others are capable of holding much larger shapes. Margaret O'Rorke, who works in England, uses 'Audrey Blackman's porcelain' (see the List of Suppliers on pages 110–11), and frequently throws forms between 35 cm (14 in) and 46 cm (18 in) high.

PREPARATION

A de-airing pug mill is invaluable if you regularly throw large quantities of porcelain, as sections of the pug can be cut to size and thrown without further preparation. For most people, who do not have access to such equipment, however, porcelain must be carefully prepared so that it is free of lumps and air and the right consistency for throwing, in order to minimize warping, bloating and cracking. This requires a combination of wedging, kneading and,

sometimes, damping to bring it to a workable state. Check before you start that your worksurfaces, wheel and tools are clean, to avoid contamination.

Unlike most other clays, some porcelains are thixotropic, and become hard when they are allowed to stand or have been filter-pressed. Before deciding to dampen hard porcelain, you should therefore *bang the clay firmly and repeatedly* on a solid surface to counteract thixotropy, and the porcelain will suddenly become more plastic and soft.

If you find that the clay is still too stiff after this, it will then need damping down before you can use it. A quick method for damping firm porcelain is to cut the clay into thick slices, press in holes with your fingers, fill them with water and then re-stack the slices. Leave the clay for about half an hour, and you will then be able to wedge and knead it. If the clay is even harder, you can pack the slices closely in a container and cover them with water, but watch them carefully as they can easily go too far, disintegrating and becoming too sloppy to prepare. The easiest method for damping porcelain, requiring less vigilance, is to wrap the hard clay in clean, wet cloths followed by several layers of polythene, and to leave it overnight, re-wetting and re-wrapping if necessary.

WEDGING

Wedging is particularly useful for amalgamating new clays of different dampnesses quickly, or for reclaimed clay which has hard lumps and sticky slips in the same piece. Wedging is extremely efficient when carried out correctly by *doubling the number of layers each time.*

Use a strong wire to cut the clay in half *vertically* on a sturdy, slightly porous surface. Stack one half on top of the other by lifting it high and then bringing it down firmly, allowing gravity as well as your energy to add force so that the two pieces of clay, and any lumps, are squashed and flattened. Free the stack from the surface with a quick jerking movement, and reposition it so that the next vertical cut is at right angles to the previous one. Repeat the procedure of cutting, pounding and stacking the clay, doubling the number of layers each time. Just ten 'cut-and-stack' operations will create a thousand layers of hard and soft clay, and as many as half a million layers after a further ten cuts! When the layers and any lumps are thin and finely dispersed, the clay is ready for kneading.

KNEADING

Porcelain which is almost ready to use, or has been wedged, will require kneading to complete the preparation. Kneading finally disperses any remaining lumps and bubbles, and aligns and compresses the particles, making the porcelain easier to use. It also counteracts thixotropy (see page 25).

The height of your worksurface is important for kneading; it should be level with your wrists when your hands are at your

Wedging. Porcelain after ten 'cut-and-stack' operations. This is a very efficient way of mixing two clays of different dampness, or for mixing or modifying body colours

sides. This will allow the whole weight of your body, working from the feet, to act on the clay, reducing the strain on your shoulders and wrists. Kneading is a little like bread-making; the weight and rhythm of the body press down through the heels of the hands on to the clay in a rocking motion. With each rocking motion, the clay is lifted back towards you and your hands move slightly further on from their finishing point before pressing down again.

Porcelain which is too soft can be formed into fat bridge shapes and left to stiffen in the air. Beware of stiffening porcelain by kneading it on plaster for a long time; this can counteract 'ageing', making the porcelain short and crumbly.

THROWING

Porcelain tends to be a 'thirsty' clay, absorbing water rapidly and then collapsing, and so many potters throw with slightly firmer clay and thin porcelain slip instead of water, in order to counteract this tendency. Slip is less easily absorbed than water and clings to the pot for longer, allowing more time for throwing and lessening the likelihood of collapse. However, for low, wide forms using large amounts of clay, which can be difficult to centre, softer porcelain is easier to use because it is not thrown high and is therefore much less likely to collapse.

The initial stages of centring, opening out

porcelain thickly, and then refine and thin the forms by turning. This is useful for creating precise forms and for minimizing warping, but the extra turning takes time and can give the work a mechanical feeling. Less-plastic porcelain bodies can be thrown thinly, using a combination of drying to remove excess slurry and stretching with a throwing stick on the inside to complete the shape.

Bamboo knives, flexible scrapers and fine wooden ribs can all be used to dry the surface gently and to stretch and complete the form,

The use of a metal kidney to gently stretch and dry the rim of a bowl

and starting to throw porcelain are similar to other clays, although porcelain generally requires a more sensitive touch and a slower pace than other bodies. However, the methods for continuing and finishing the throwing process can take different directions.

Some skilled potters work freely, handling porcelain in the same way as other clays but keeping the wetting to a minimum, and producing forms with a spontaneous and natural feeling. Other potters throw the

Throwing with an improvised egote *tool, made from a wooden spoon, to stretch and throw the inside of a narrow-necked teapot*

Lifting a freshly thrown shape from the wheel, using two strips of newspaper folded double

smoothing the surface at the same time to minimize finger marks. A throwing stick (or the Japanese *egote*), which has a smooth, curved blob on the end, is used to stretch tall, enclosed forms such as teapots or vases from the inside (see photograph, left). An *egote* can also be used to 'pull up' the wall of a pot, with the other hand working against it from outside.

Whatever your approach to throwing, using batts will reduce the porcelain's tendency to warp and collapse. Batts are essential when large pieces or flat plates and dishes are thrown. However, small bowls and cylindrical forms can be removed from the wheel using newspaper; this will lessen the likelihood of the soft pots being damaged by fingermarks or 'ovaling' (see photograph, page 27).

THROWING PLATES, WIDE FORMS AND UNUSUAL SHAPES

Porcelain plates, and other shapes with wide bases, can develop S-shaped cracks during drying. Compressing the base as firmly as possible during throwing with the edge of the hand or a robust wooden rib will help to counteract this, as will slow, even drying. The rims of plates and saucers also present problems, often springing upward as they dry: this is known as 'plastic memory'. Experience and observation will reveal the difference between over-stretching and drying the rim with a rib, which seems to exacerbate plastic memory, and throwing for too long so that the rim becomes too wet and soft, causing it to collapse.

Plastic memory also causes thrown teapot spouts to twist out of alignment during the glaze firing. This can be prevented by cutting the end of the spout at a slight angle once the spout has been joined to the body. Position the teapot with the spout pointing towards you, and cut the left-hand side of the spout slightly lower than the right side, so that the cut is not quite horizontal. (This process must be reversed and the spout cut lower on the

Using a single sheet of uncreased newspaper to retain the shape of a bowl when removing it from the wheel. The rim is wetted to seal the newspaper to the pot and therefore to trap the air inside

right side if you are throwing 'oriental style', with the wheel travelling clockwise.)

Throwing certain extreme shapes in porcelain can be attempted by collaring in the top and completely enclosing the form. The air trapped inside the pot allows it to be shaped or strongly angled using ribs and metal kidneys. You can make boxes in this way, without making and measuring a separate lid, by using a small, square-ended

tool to press gently into the clay to form a gallery and rim at an appropriate place (often at the mid-point between the base and the top). When the box is leather-hard, pierce a small hole in the gallery to allow the air inside – now under compression – to escape. Separate the lid and base when they are leather-hard by turning with a pin to free the lid. Finally, turn both parts of the box to fit and to finish the shape, making a footring if necessary.

A fine, twisted wire is best for cutting porcelain off the wheel, as single wires simply allow the fine porcelain base to stick back on to the smooth layer of clay beneath. Porcelain has a tendency to dry suddenly and unevenly, so it is vital to place thrown work where it can dry slowly, away from draughts. Rims can often dry before bases, so you should wrap the pots in soft polythene to allow the rims and bases to equalize in dampness. The pots can then be turned with less chance of cracking at the rim. I cannot emphasize enough how important it is to minimize warping by allowing *any* work in porcelain to equalize in dampness in this way, before turning or joining, and then to dry slowly and evenly away from draughts and heat.

Although the basis of throwing could be said to consist of variations on three forms – the bowl, the cylinder and the plate – there is still tremendous scope for creating complex forms by combining two or more pieces. This is especially useful for porcelain, where large or complex forms are difficult to throw in a single piece. You can experiment further by combining techniques: throwing a pot thickly and faceting the walls using a cutting wire; squashing and ovaling; or patting and padding.

Joining forms when they are soft tends to result in fluid lines, but when they are leather-hard more articulated forms can be created. Thrown components can be used upside down or turned on their sides to make surprising forms. Bear in mind that good thrown sections and accurate joins are important, because porcelain is more sensitive than other clays to stresses set up in the form, which can twist and warp in the firing.

It is advisable to have a clear idea of the form from the start, as porcelain can change dramatically with each stage of throwing, turning and assembling. Sketches can help you to work out ideas quickly, and you can then refer to these when checking proportions of components during the making. In order to develop the creative process, it is also important to relinquish old ideas and methods and to experiment with new ones. It is surprising how refreshing it can be to work in a completely different way – perhaps very quickly – without worrying about the end result, but being determined to enjoy yourself!

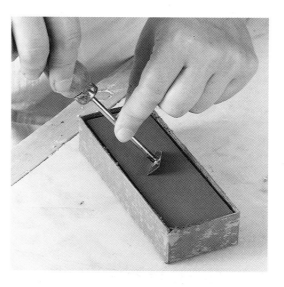

Tool sharpening. Using a sharpening stone with light oil as a lubricant. The tool is held at an angle of about 45° and carefully rubbed back and forth over the stone

Using a mirror to show the profile of the form while throwing or turning. The mirror should be suitably angled so that the thrower can see the form in profile without having to bend over

TURNING

Turning, and the skills associated with turning, play an important part in the form and finish of thrown porcelain. This is not only because porcelain is often thrown thickly, but because its material qualities are such that the whole surface may be turned, allowing simple and shapely profiles to emerge. A smooth surface may serve as a foundation for decoration, or to create a particular relationship between the sensuousness of the glaze and the smoothness of the body (although some porcelain does bear throwing marks as part of its character and design).

Translucence – for many the most notable characteristic of porcelain – is achieved by skilful turning, as more light is transmitted through a thinner section. Turning a fine section may require removing the work from the wheel several times to check the thickness, accurately re-centring the pot each time so that the section remains even.

It is very satisfying to turn porcelain when it is at just the right stage of firmness and the clay springs away from the tool in long, snaking ribbons. If the clay is too damp, however, it will clog up the tool, and the pressure will distort the shape easily. When the work is too dry, the porcelain turns off in flakes, and pressure from the tool may start hairline cracks at the rim. For the best results it is vital to keep your tools well-sharpened (see page 29), so that they cut as efficiently as possible. It is also important to keep the wheel moving at a brisk pace when turning. Extra-flexible steel kidneys (or scrapers) are especially useful for smoothing the surface of porcelain, and a selection of very small loop tools (used by modellers for hollowing clay forms) will enable you to turn fine detail.

ATTACHING WORK TO THE WHEEL

There are many ways of attaching work to the wheel for turning, and each potter will adapt and vary these to suit their needs. The simplest method is to centre the pot and secure it to the wheel using soft coils or wads of porcelain placed around the rim. These coils prevent the turning of the whole surface, but this can be remedied by using a thin layer of slip to stick the rim of the pot on to a

Turning a pot upright, before inverting it to complete the footring. The pot is stuck to the wheel with slip

fairly smooth but slightly porous batt (made of materials such as plastic, perspex, masonite or hardboard). You can also make a smooth surface on textured batts, such as plywood, by coating the surface with a thin layer of high-density plaster. You must avoid scratching this surface, however, or the flakes of plaster will contaminate the turnings. If the work is a little dry for turning, damping with a spray will help, but beware of over-wetting dry porcelain or blisters may form. These will then subside, only to reappear after the glaze firing!

I prefer to begin turning with the pot the right way up, sticking the base of the pot to the batt with slip and then compressing and sealing it to the batt with a rounded wooden tool. Turning a pot the right way up makes it easier to assess its profile, and to check the section by touch without removing it from the wheel. It also enables some of the weight to be turned away from large, shallow forms and those with delicate rims, before inverting them to complete the foot.

Porcelain pots with very fine or uneven rims can be turned on a hump of clay, so that the rim is freed from contact with the batt. A small square of fine clean cotton stretched over the hump will prevent damp pots from slipping or sticking. The humps can be re-used if you keep them damp by wrapping them in plastic. Using tall humps raises the height at which turning takes place, reducing back strain from bending over the work, while a cylinder or 'chuck' of leather-hard clay can be used to support long or narrow-necked pieces at the shoulder. Sophisticated grips are also available, especially in the USA, which not only hold complex forms in place but centre them as well.

In my opinion, however, the quickest way to centre work repeatedly is to master 'tap centring'. Watching someone tap centre pots for turning makes it look so quick and easy, but patient practice is needed to acquire the skill. Once you have mastered this technique, you will be able to remove pots from the wheel frequently to check the thickness and speedily re-centre them, so it is particularly appropriate for porcelain, where a fine section is sought. Tap centring has the added advantage of allowing any part of the pot to be centred. How often have you noticed that some pots, although centred at the rim, are knocking out of true at the base where you want to turn?

To practise tap centring, do not worry too much about placing the pot centrally; it is easier to check the effectiveness of your tapping if you begin off-centre with the wheel at a medium speed. Press the middle finger of your left hand on the base at the 'still point', and then, with the other hand, rhythmically tap the right side of the pot where it is strongest, near the foot, using the side of your hand (palm upward) or your fingertips. Experiment by tapping more firmly and softly, and by altering the speed of the wheel and the rhythm of the tapping.

If the pot is moving too far with each tap, try increasing the pressure of your left hand (which is holding the pot down) or hitting more gently. The nearer the pot is to being centred, the gentler the tapping should be. One thing is certain: if you 'think' about centring the pot and try to hit the part that sticks out, by the time your hand has received the message from your brain, the bulge will have moved on! If you *must* 'think', try to imagine the wheel as a clockface. When the bulge appears at 10 o'clock, immediately tap at 3 or 4 o'clock. Not all potters tap with their right hand – some use their left hand at 7 o'clock, regardless of the direction of the wheel.

Jenny Beavan *Porcelain bottle.*
Hand-built, height 45 cm (17¾in)

CHAPTER FOUR

HAND-BUILDING AND MODELLING

Porcelain is a surprisingly versatile material for hand-building. It can be slabbed, pinched, modelled or coiled, or worked with a combination of these methods. Few potters coil with porcelain, however, possibly because the coils show up as slight corrugations after firing and also because of the difficulty of getting a good bond between the coils.

JOINING

Many of the problems encountered in joining porcelain are due to its high shrinkage rate or to uneven or sudden drying, when cracks may occur. For the best results, the pieces to be joined should be of equal dampness and formed for an accurate fit. Score both of the surfaces to be joined with a blade or pin, and join them using porcelain slip. You can make the slip by slaking dry body scraps in hot water and sieving them into an airtight container. Margaret O'Rorke recommends the use of vinegar for joining, while other potters just use water and persistent scoring. Remember, too, that vinegar slip is useful for mending cracks.

It is inevitable that some pieces to be joined will not be of equal dampness: for example, modelled details or handles and knobs that are pulled or thrown directly on to leather-hard work. You should take extra care to dry these pieces slowly by wrapping them in polythene. A coating of wax over the join will help to slow the drying and to prevent cracking, especially on handles.

SLABBING

Slabbed porcelain can be used on its own or with press-moulds to make almost any kind of form, from plates, vases, dishes and tiles to sculpture. It can be miniature in scale or very grand (see the photograph on page 34). The firmness or plasticity of the slabs, which need skilful handling, can produce starkly geometric or soft and sensuous forms, depending on your designs and intentions.

Porcelain slabs – whether glazed or unglazed – have a smooth, white surface for decoration, and complex patterns and textures can be built up on the slabs before they are cut to shape and joined (see the photograph on page 32).

MAKING SLABS

Porcelain is sensitive to the way that it is handled, and so an even, methodical approach to making slabs will prevent excessive bulging and warping in the finished work from stress caused during the making.

You can make large quantities of slabs quickly using a clay harp. This is a wide, U-shaped piece of metal with a wire stretched across the mouth. It is used to cut horizontally through a block of clay by progressively moving the wire up the notches on the harp. Alternatively, by leaving the wire on the lowest notch, you can cut the slabs one at a time. You can create interesting textures by pulling strongly twisted wire (such as springs which have been stretched)

each pass to minimize stress from the rolling.

You can roll very thin sheets of porcelain between clean sheets of polythene. This prevents the sheets from drying out during rolling and makes them easier to move. This is also a valuable method for inlay work: complex patterns can be built up over days, if necessary, without the slab drying out.

STORING SLABS

Porcelain slabs require careful and even drying if you intend to use them when they are leather-hard. You can lay them on absorbent boards and turn them frequently, but this requires constant monitoring. By creating a controlled environment using polythene, newspaper and boards, you will be able to gradually stiffen or keep your porcelain slabs moist as required. You can stack multiple slabs with ten or twelve sheets of newspaper between each slab, wrapping them in polythene on a flat board, but irregularly shaped slabs are less likely to warp if they are stored on separate boards and not on top of each other.

JOINING SLABS

When the slabs are sufficiently stiff, cut them to size with a fine, sharp knife. Unless you

Masamichi Yoshikawa 'Orebes Changed into White'. *Slabbed porcelain, 30 × 30 × 15 cm (12 × 12 × 6 in)*

through the porcelain in a series of curves. A similar method involves using a wire stretched between two evenly notched sticks, pulled strongly apart to keep the tension on the wire. The size of the harp and the block of clay limit the slabs to a modest size; larger slabs must be made by rolling.

Hand-rolling is the simplest method for small slabs, using a rolling pin, a clean dry cloth and two guide sticks of the required thickness to support the ends of the rolling pin. Roll out the porcelain on the cloth, thinning it gradually and turning the cloth frequently so that the slab is rolled in different directions to minimize rolling stress. To prevent the porcelain from sticking or tearing, use a fresh, dry cloth for each slab.

A mechanical slab roller makes the task of rolling large slabs much less of an effort than rolling by hand. Place the porcelain between clean cloths and 'wind' it through the rollers (not unlike an old-fashioned clothes wringer), turning the clay 'sandwich' through 90° with

Right: ***Dorothy Hafner*** *'Flic-flac'. Hand-painted porcelain punchbowl with ladle, 23 × 33 × 33 cm (9 × 13 × 13 in)*

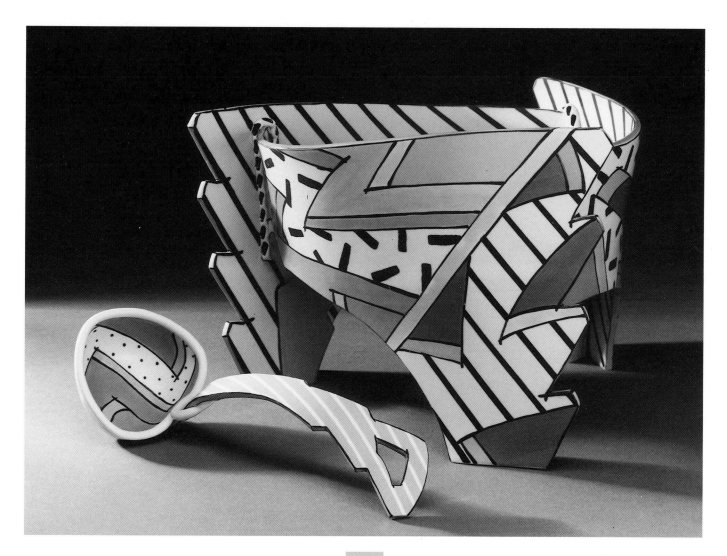

will be using them soft, avoid cutting slabs in the plastic state because they are more likely to stretch when you lift them, and will dry more quickly at the edges and be liable to curl. Templates save time when cutting repeated shapes, and these can be made from paper, cardboard or polythene. Waterproof tar paper from builders' merchants makes excellent templates, which can be left in contact with the porcelain to support the form while it stiffens.

A little excess slurry squeezing out from the join when you press it together is a sign that you have used enough slip, and that the joint is less likely to part. You can wipe away this slurry using a natural sponge or a damp brush. A coil of soft porcelain smoothed over the inside of the join will help to prevent the slabs from cracking and springing apart. You must dry slabbed porcelain slowly and evenly, away from draughts and supported where necessary with clay or foam rubber. Wrap the work in polythene to ensure the dampness equalizes throughout.

PINCHING

Pinching is a technique often taught to beginners as an introduction to handling clay. Although it is an excellent way of comparing the working qualities of different bodies, it requires persistence, observation and experience to develop the skills and sensitivity necessary to achieve satisfactory forms. Handled skilfully, porcelain is particularly

suitable for pinching because of its smoothness and strength when it is very thin. Mary Rogers's book *On Pottery and Porcelain* (see the Bibliography on page 109) is an excellent source of inspiration and information about pinching.

EXPLORING PINCHING

Begin with a small ball of porcelain that fits comfortably into the palm of your hand. Holding the ball with one hand, use your other hand to pinch, with your thumb at the top of the clay and your fingers at the base. Pinch rhythmically, and gradually turn the ball. Press your thumb downward to make a hole in the clay until the base is the correct thickness. Then, with the form inverted, slowly and rhythmically pinch in circles, or a spiral, from the base to the rim.

Pinching is a very gradual process, and the clay often becomes too soft or too stiff to continue, so wrap or spray the work as necessary. Using just your fingertips, rather than your palms, will help to slow the drying, and a little cooking oil rubbed into your fingers will keep the porcelain workable for longer. Over-working the form can make it floppy, so it should be set aside to stiffen before this happens. Pinching the clay with the form inverted or cupped on its side counteracts the tendency for it to 'pancake'. The form can be stiffened on its rim while you work on another pot, or stored in a cup or on a coil of clay if the rim is too fragile.

Pinching too hard will cause cracks at the

rim of a pot, so you must decide whether these enhance the form or are unsightly and weaken the structure. You can prevent cracks from appearing by compressing the rim and keeping it damp or trimmed using a sharp blade or scissors, and smoothing it with a damp chamois leather.

You can increase the size of a pinched form by stroking the clay from the inside to stretch the form, by enlarging it beyond the depth of your fingers, by combining two or more forms, or by adding feet. As a general rule, however, the scale of pinched work is naturally small, and invites close scrutiny of the surface and form. Be prepared to select the best pots rigorously and to reject those that are unsatisfactory.

The surface of a pot may appear dimpled from the pinching; you can remove this dimpling when the porcelain is leather-hard by scraping gently with a fine-toothed hacksaw blade and metal kidney. (Wear a face-mask to prevent the inhalation of dust.) Alternatively, you can sand the pot after biscuit firing.

MODELLING

From the very earliest times, people have used clay to model figures and animals and to embellish pots. Porcelain was found to be particularly suitable for these purposes, with its whiteness and fineness making it ideal for creating crisp, clear detail and colourful decoration. Today, a small group of people

use porcelain for modelling, often developing personal techniques which characterize their work. The most successful designs display a strong sense of proportion, and are informed by a knowledge of drawing and observation rather than by the inclusion of minute detail. What is *left out* rather than what is included makes the work more than mere reproduction in miniature; in other words it is 'essence rather than actuality'. Audrey Blackman's book, *Rolled Pottery Figures* (see the Bibliography on page 109) illustrates this well.

APPROACHES TO MODELLING

Porcelain can be modelled in a solid state and then hollowed, or made hollow from the beginning, using slabbing, coiling or throwing to create a structure for modelling. Almost any form can be modelled in porcelain, but it should be designed so that it is compact and as self-supporting as possible, because the clay softens at its maturing temperature and is inclined to bend and crack. A good selection of boxwood modelling tools is essential for fine detailing, as are wire-loop tools for carving and hollowing. Soft brushes and a chamois leather are useful for smoothing and tidying the surfaces.

When modelling solid porcelain, you can add or remove clay until the form is almost

Ruth Barrett-Danes 'Guardian Vessel'. *Porcelain with* terra sigillata *colours, height 22 cm (8½in)*

complete, but remember that porcelain will only adhere to itself using pressure alone when it is very soft; otherwise it should be slipped and scored. Solid-formed sculpture dries less quickly than hollow-formed sculpture, which is an advantage with porcelain. However, it will gradually slump, and later, when you become aware that everything is out of proportion, the porcelain form is often too stiff to alter. You therefore need to check and correct the sculpture at frequent intervals as it stiffens. Knitting needles pierced through the modelling at strategic points (such as a spine) will help to prevent slumping, but remove them before the work becomes too hard. Columns of clay (separated from the form with newspaper) or foam rubber make excellent supports, because they shrink with the form as it dries.

When the modelled porcelain is leather-hard, and before you have added too much detail, you must cut it in half with a fine wire and hollow out the interior with a wire-loop tool. Complex forms may need more than one cut. A couple of marks scored lightly over the cut will help you to relocate the pieces once you have hollowed them out. You can re-model the sculpture and add any details once you have joined the halves.

Emily Myers *Biscuit porcelain forms with extruded rims*

Check the section with a pin to ensure that it does not exceed 2 cm (¾ in) in thickness and is of even thickness throughout. The difficulty with firing thicker porcelain is that the heat may not completely penetrate the work in the early stages, and this stress can lead to shattering as chemically combined water in the interior is released as steam. Pierce a small hole through to the hollow area to allow the air to escape during firing.

With hollow-forming techniques, the underlying form has to stiffen sufficiently before you add the detail (a hairdryer can speed up the drying process). You must also check the thickness where you have modelled extra porcelain into the form. Hollow forms tend to dry quickly, even when wrapped, and a common problem is keeping the work both sufficiently damp to receive additions of soft clay, but firm enough to continue building. Placing damp sponges in the polythene will help to slow down the drying process. Drape fine details, which are vulnerable to drying, with soft polythene or a damp cloth while you are working other areas. It is almost inevitable that when you have finished modelling some areas will be drier than others, so it is vital to wrap the piece in polythene and store it until it has had time to equalize.

You should fire animals and other forms which will stand on legs, or on several small points, on a separate slab of porcelain made from the same body and bedded on placing powder. This slab of porcelain will shrink at the same rate as the model, preventing it from cracking as a result of dragging or sticking on the kiln shelf. For unglazed models, you can make supports from the porcelain, or sometimes from ceramic fibre, and use them to prop the work while it is fired.

EXTRUDING

An extruder, whether electrical or hand-powered, is an extremely versatile addition to the workshop. Extruders work by forcing clay, held in a barrel, through a die. The die may have a single hole or a series of holes to shape the clay as it is forced through. Ready-made dies are sold in fairly standard shapes, such as coils or straps for handles and rims, but metal blanks are available so that you can design your own shapes. Alternatively, they can be cut from sheets of perspex. The holes must be distributed as symmetrically as possible on the die so that the extruded clay comes out evenly, and is less likely to curve. Dies can also be designed to form hollow extrusions, which can be large enough – with the inclusion of an expansion box – to form vessels.

You must clean the extruder each time for really smooth results, and prepare the porcelain very well so that it is free of air bubbles. Trapped air in the clay annoyingly emerges from the extruder as burst air bubbles, which can cause the extrusion to fall apart or crack when bent, although 10 per cent of fine molochite added to the porcelain will help to prevent cracking on extrusions. If the molochite is coarse, the edges will tear, which can give a decorative effect.

Ruth Barret-Danes *'Fleeing Pig'. Modelled porcelain, height 26 cm (10 in)*

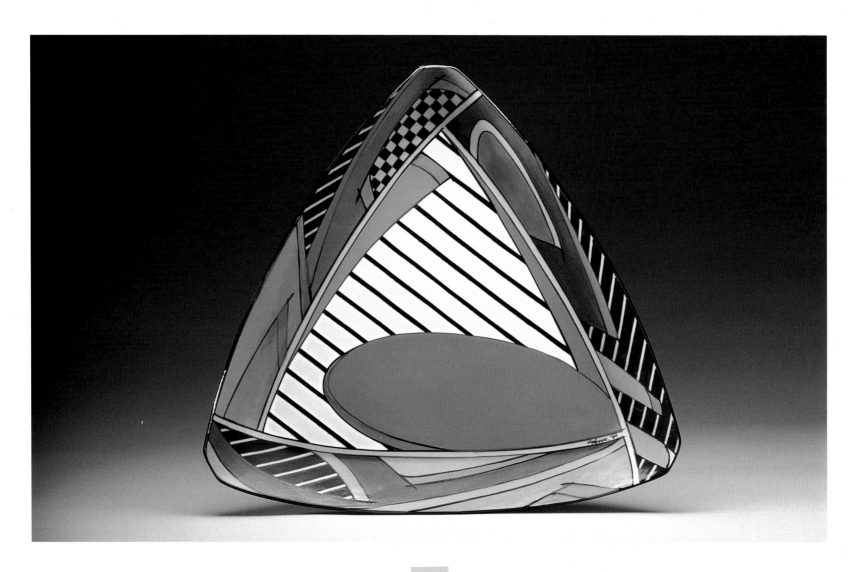

CHAPTER FIVE

MOULDS

During the 1960s and '70s there was a widespread rejection of industrial processes by studio potters in the Western world. This is now changing, however, and there is a growing interest from some potters in the industrial techniques of slip-casting and press-moulding, although opinions on moulds remain sharply divided. There are those who regard moulds and their associated techniques with mistrust, linking them to the production of sterile forms which lack individuality or life, while other potters have reclaimed the mould as a valuable 'tool', and use it creatively to make repeated forms which they then decorate and embellish individually. Moulds may also be used to make modules, which are assembled to create complex forms. For coloured porcelain agate ware or

Left: *Dorothy Hafner* '*Pink Disc*'. *Press-moulded porcelain tray, 43 × 43 × 5 cm (17 × 17 × 2 in)*. Photograph by Baker Vail

inlaid porcelain, where the decoration is integral to the forming process, moulds assist in forming and supporting the work as it stiffens.

Moulds can be either convex or concave. When hollow, they are used for press-moulding and slip-casting, while hump moulds produce forms when clay is draped or pressed over the mould. Simple shapes without undercuts are made in a single piece mould, while complex shapes may need several interlocking pieces to form a mould, which then has to be taken apart to release the clay form.

Plaster of Paris is most commonly used for making moulds. It is an extremely smooth material, and is capable of reproducing fine detail. The most useful characteristic of plaster is its microporous nature, which gives it great absorbency. This encourages the clay or slip to dry quickly and to shrink from the mould, thus freeing the form.

The potter Joanna Howells uses an oval plaster mould to alter the shape of her

thrown dishes, which retain the throwing marks as a decorative clue to the initial forming process (see photographs, page 42). She throws the feet separately, and allows them to stiffen a little before she cuts them from the batt. She then gently squeezes the feet into oval forms before joining them to the oval moulded dish. (For the sake of speed, Joanna prefers to join the feet *after* biscuit firing, glazing the foot ring and dish separately. She then carefully places them together in the kiln so that they are bonded by the molten glaze.)

You can use found objects such as bricks or pebbles to make hump moulds for shallow forms, as well as wood, which you can cut to a suitable shape. Any form made over a hump mould must be released before it shrinks on to the mould and cracks vertically at the rim. This is a particular problem with porcelain, because it shrinks more than other clays and – even when apparently stiff – tends to be floppy and to become distorted when handled.

Below left: **Joanna Howells** *A freely thrown disc of porcelain is cut from the wheel and placed on an oval plaster mould. The excess clay at the edges is trimmed away with a potter's knife*

Centre: *The mould is firmly banged on a towel. This protects it and allows the freshly thrown porcelain to stretch into the mould*

Right: *The rim of the dish is trimmed to the edge of the mould and smoothed with a rubber kidney. When the dish is leather-hard, the rim is cut to the shape seen on the finished dish in the background*

Contemporary materials such as expanded polystyrene or styrofoam can be cut into complex dish moulds. Although they are much less absorbent than plaster, they have the advantage of being many times lighter, and are therefore easier to store and handle. Shapes with sloping sides can be cut using a jigsaw with a variable-angled blade. You will need to make a separate base for these moulds, because the jigsaw must cut right through the polystyrene to release the central part, which you can then use as a hump mould. A wooden board can serve as a base for the hollow mould, and will allow you to press out the completed form from below.

PRESS MOULDS

You can form the simplest type of mould by suspending a cloth from the legs of a chair or stool and securing it with string. This type of 'hammock' mould is useful for making free-formed shapes. Place a slab of soft clay, already cut to shape or left free-form, in the hammock and then stroke and coax it into shape with a rubber kidney.

When you are making shallow forms such as dishes and bowls, especially if they are not in the round, you will find that press moulds are quick and easy to use. By combining these moulded forms in pairs, it is possible to make

more complex or enclosed shapes such as vases and bottles (see photograph, page 44).

To prepare porcelain for pressing into moulds you must first roll out the clay evenly on a clean cloth. This slab should be about 2–3 cm ($\frac{1}{2}$–1 in) wider than the top edge of the mould for shallow moulds, and larger still for deeper moulds. You must lift the porcelain very carefully from the rolling cloth so that it is not stretched, or it will distort in the firing. I use one hand on either side of the slab and gently ease it upward, away from the cloth. Then I gently place the slab on top of the press mould. Hold the edge of the slab with your fingertips and, lifting the slab upwards, press it carefully into the mould. Move your hands on a little further round the mould each time you lift and press. Avoid over-working the porcelain, or it will develop stress cracks where it has been handled too much.

A rubber kidney is invaluable for smoothing the surface of the slab and for finally pressing it into contact with the mould. It requires practice to create a smooth, line-free surface – some potters prefer to use a dampened natural sponge for this purpose. You can then trim away the

Derek Davis 'The Kiss'. *Hammock-moulded and cut to shape, 53 × 35.5 × 8 cm (21 × 14 × 3$\frac{1}{4}$in)*

Russell Coates
Press-moulded vase.
Porcelain with underglaze
and enamels, height 19 cm
(7½in)

excess porcelain using a thin, sharp blade held parallel to the top of the mould. Take care not to cut downwards on to the surface of the mould, as you may damage it, and small pieces of plaster will contaminate the clay. Once you have trimmed the excess clay, you can add rims and handles while the form is still in the mould.

Provided that the moulds are not damp from repeated use, the pressed forms will dry and shrink quite quickly. Porcelain warps so easily, however, that it is important not to remove the clay from the mould when it is too soft. Handle the form by supporting it equally at either side, as any tension set up within the clay will reappear as warping once it has been fired.

BISCUITED MOULDS AND SPRIG MOULDS

Before the discovery of plaster of Paris, biscuited clay was used to make reasonably porous and very durable moulds. These biscuit moulds were used in China more than a thousand years ago, and are still employed today.

Porcelain is a particularly good mould material. Being a very smooth clay, it is capable of reproducing fine detail, and can be carved when leather-hard into stamps and seals (for impressed decoration), and also pressed with found objects to make sprig

moulds. Items such as shells and nuts, manufactured objects such as buttons or metalwork, and even biscuited porcelain shapes can be used to make biscuit sprig moulds. However, biscuit sprig moulds can only be made by pressing reasonably strong objects into plastic porcelain, whereas plaster sprig moulds may be cast from any object, even if it is soft.

To make a sprig mould, form a small block of porcelain that is at least 1 cm ($\frac{1}{2}$ in) larger all round than the object itself, not forgetting that this applies to the depth as well as to the width and the length. Before pressing the object into the block of plastic porcelain, a fine dusting of talc on both the clay and the object will help to ease them apart. You can also rock the object very gently to release it from the clay. With a little practice, you will be able to tell just how hard or soft the porcelain block should be, and how deep to press the object before removing it. The sprig mould must then be dried slowly and biscuited in the usual way.

Russell Coates uses a large hump mould made from biscuited porcelain to change the shape of his freshly thrown dishes to octagonal-sided dishes. He makes the mould from a very thickly thrown shallow bowl, which he cuts and shaves to shape when it is leather-hard. He adds a cylinder of leather-hard porcelain to the inside of the bowl to act as a pedestal and lift the mould above the surface of the wheelhead (see photographs on pages 46–7).

SLIP-CAST PORCELAIN

The process of slip casting is deceptively simple: liquid porcelain casting slip (see page 49) is poured into a plaster-of-Paris mould and, as the water from the slip is absorbed, a layer of porcelain is gradually built up on the surface of the mould. When this layer of clay reaches the required thickness, the mould is inverted and the surplus slip drained out. The cast is removed from the mould when it is firm, and is then finally trimmed and finished.

In spite of the simplicity, however, the design and making of moulds and the formulation and mixing of casting slip are very exacting processes. Time and research are needed to obtain satisfactory, repeatable results. It is not possible in this book to give an in-depth explanation of slip-cast porcelain, although some general guidelines can be given for making porcelain slip. (For further advice on the design and making of moulds, refer to the Bibliography on page 109.)

As increasing numbers of potters are using porcelain to slip-cast forms, manufacturers have started to produce porcelain casting slip (see the List of Suppliers on pages 110–11). Most suppliers will give advice on recipes for mixing porcelain casting slip, using their plastic or powdered porcelain bodies. Not all plastic porcelain bodies are suitable for making casting slip, however, as some of them contain bentonite, which can cause excessive warping in cast shapes.

Russell Coates *The centred biscuit mould is fixed to the wheel with coils of soft porcelain*

A freshly thrown porcelain bowl, still stuck to its throwing batt, is carefully lowered on to the eight-sided biscuit mould

After cutting from the batt, the soft porcelain pot is pressed gently on to the biscuit mould, as the wheel revolves slowly

The rim of the bowl is trimmed close to the edge of the mould with a wire, while the wheel revolves slowly

When the dish has stiffened a little, it is turned carefully in order to form a foot

The mould and dish are inverted, and the mould is then released carefully to reveal the form

A good, workable casting slip should not shrink too much from wet to leather-hard, and it must have good *dry* strength. It must remain in suspension without settling out, and, most importantly, must be sufficiently fluid to pour into and out of the mould using a minimum amount of water aided by a deflocculant. The fluidity of a casting slip is related to several factors: the type and the amount of deflocculant, the water and the plastic clay. The addition of the deflocculant causes the electrically charged clay particles to repel each other. This has the dramatic effect of making a very thick slip suddenly fluid, with the result that it requires much less water to be pourable. A deflocculated slip also *shrinks* far less because of the lowered water content. Deflocculants rarely amount to more than 0.5 per cent of the dry weight of the ingredients, as too much deflocculant will make the cast difficult to trim.

Soda ash and sodium silicate are the most commonly used deflocculants, either individually or in the ratio of 1:3. Too much sodium silicate makes the cast brittle, but it has the advantage of decreasing thixotropy, which occurs when the slip thickens after standing. Do not thin down thickened slip with water, but thoroughly blunge or mix it. If it is still thick after it has been thoroughly mixed, you can add a tiny amount of extra deflocculant to thin it.

Pottery suppliers also sell ready-mixed deflocculants (see pages 110–11). 'Dispex' is available in the UK, and 'Darvan 7', an

Sasha Wardell *Slip-cast, semi-porcelain teapot, height 18 cm (7¼in). Teacups, bone china, height 8 cm (3¼in). Both teapot and cups have airbrushed decoration*

American product, is valuable because it is not easily absorbed into the mould. The absorbency and therefore the working life of a mould are prolonged when the micropores do not become quickly filled with dissolved materials (mostly deflocculants).

The water content of a porcelain casting slip should not exceed 50 per cent by weight of the dry ingredients, and may be as low as 25 per cent. A lower water content allows more castings to be taken from a mould before it becomes saturated, and means that fewer dissolved materials are absorbed into the plaster. The hardness or softness of the water will affect the amount of deflocculant needed to make the slip fluid. Water containing chlorine will require more deflocculant.

The plastic ingredients in the slip, such as ball clay and bentonite, should not exceed half the total dry weight of the ingredients. Ball clay is used in slips to increase dry strength, and because it is a colloid. Clay particles of less than 0.5 micrometres help to form colloids, enabling the particles to remain in suspension. Slips should contain a range of particle sizes, which enables the particles to pack together, so that less water is needed to make the slip fluid. Ball clay also contains organic matter which, as it increases in a recipe, requires a corresponding increase in alkaline deflocculant in order to keep the slip fluid.

MIXING CASTING SLIP

Porcelain body recipes make a useful starting point for mixing casting slips, but the quantity of ball clay will probably have to be lowered and the bentonite may not be needed at all. As when mixing porcelain bodies, you should add the ingredients to the measured amount of water, beginning with the most plastic and ending with the least plastic ingredient; the ratio of water to dry material will result in a very stiff mixture. Mix the deflocculant in a little hot water, taken from the total amount calculated for the slip, and add this to the mixed ingredients *drop by drop* while you blunge it. If possible, you should measure the specific gravity of the slip, using a hydrometer, and record it so that you can make consistent batches of slip.

When mixing a recipe for the first time, do not add *all* the measured water or dissolved deflocculant at once – the slip may become fluid without using the total amount. If you are trying a new recipe, it is possible to work out how much deflocculant you need by using 1 kg (2.2 lb) of dry ingredients to not more than 450 ml (15 fl oz) of water (do not add all this at once, as it may not all be needed). Then take 100 ml (3.4 fl oz) of hot water, and add 2.5 g (0.08 oz) of soda ash and 7.5 g (0.26 oz) of sodium silicate, and mix them thoroughly.

Add most of the allowance of water to the dry ingredients and then introduce the dissolved deflocculant, drop by drop, until the slip is fluid (you should need more than half of this mixture). Note the amount of deflocculant left over in ml (fl oz) and subtract this from the original 100 ml (3.4 fl oz); each 10 ml (0.3 fl oz) of mixture that you use is equivalent to 1 g (0.04 oz) of deflocculant.

Geoffrey Eastop: porcelain casting slip

China clay	5.9 kg	(13 lb)
Flint	2.04 kg	(4.5 lb)
Potash feldspar	3.29 kg	(7.25 lb)
B.B.V. ball clay	1.36 kg	(3 lb)
Bentonite	0.23 kg	(8 oz)
Sodium silicate	32 g	(1.13 oz)
Hot water	6.82 l	(12 pt)

Dorothy Hafner: porcelain casting slip (Cone 7)
(*Ceramics Monthly*, July–Aug. 1982)

Nepheline syenite	25
Ball clay	10
Edgar plastic kaolin	20
Kaolin (6 tile)	20
Flint	25

Note: For 227 kg (500 lb) of dry ingredients, use 102 litres (27 galls) of water, 350 cc of liquid 'N' brand soda silicate and 50 g (1.8 oz) of soda ash. The specific gravity should be adjusted to 1.76.

Joanna Veevers 'Fish Case – Natural History
Museum'. Wall piece, stained porcelain,
26 × 21 cm (10 × 8 in), 1989

CHAPTER SIX

DECORATION

Although porcelain may be admired for the beauty and simplicity of its form, in addition to the sensuous quality of its glazes, it is also noted for its decoration. The painting of underglaze blue, set against the cool, smooth background of porcelain, is universally appreciated, as are its particular qualities when it is carved and glazed with a fluid, pale-coloured glaze that pools into the detail and emphasizes the depths with different tones.

With the exception of translucence, or particular glaze effects, there is no added effect from the porcelain body itself, such as the iron spotting of a reduced stoneware. Porcelain is like a blank canvas: any decoration that you wish to achieve in the end is entirely up to you, and this can be daunting as well as rewarding. Porcelain is an exacting material to decorate: the fineness and smoothness of the body reflect the faintest mark, it dries more quickly than other clays, it cracks easily and warps when it is too soft.

Most decorative techniques can be used with porcelain, but, because of its whiteness, it is particularly suitable for colour in the body or the glaze, or as painted decoration. Porcelain is also an appropriate body for carving and cutting because of its fineness and strength, and such techniques are enhanced by the clay's unique quality of translucence. Conversely, it seems inappropriate to cloak porcelain in a glaze, or colour or handle it in such a way that its qualities are obscured.

The art of decorating requires practice in order to develop skill with the tools and create patterns, especially when the maker is faced with a large white expanse of porcelain! As porcelain demands a certain degree of accuracy and skill in decoration, it is helpful to have a way of practising decoration directly on pots, and a method for marking out areas for design before finally carrying it out. You may find food colouring useful for practising decorative techniques and for marking out those areas that are to be decorated. These painted marks gradually

Caroline Whyman decorating a porcelain vase with slip spots, using food colouring to mark out a grid with which to position the spots

fade on raw clay, so that you can make revisions before starting the decoration, and any remaining marks will burn away in the firing. Food colouring is available from most supermarkets and grocery stores in a range of colours (the darker ones will show on the surface for longer), and can be used on raw or biscuit porcelain.

PIERCING

The particular appeal of pierced porcelain is that intricate and delicate detail can be cut out of the fine walls of a pot, and yet it will remain strong after firing. With thrown forms in particular, piercing is more frequently made near the rim rather than the foot, where removal of too much clay weakens the form.

Decorative piercing and carving are best carried out when the porcelain form is quite leather-hard, so that it can be handled without losing its shape. You can continue work to the point just before the clay dries, when the body colour suddenly changes and becomes much paler. Hairline cracks are very easy to make by pressing too hard with the hands or the tools; annoyingly, they do not show until after the glaze firing.

As porcelain is rather dense when leather-hard, you must keep all your cutting or

Lizzie Bicknell *Piercing porcelain with a thin, sharp blade. The round-handled tool facilitates the cutting of the curves*

piercing tools very sharp and clean so that they cut the clay easily and smoothly without pressing too hard. You can buy some suitable tools from pottery suppliers (see pages 110–11), but many general pottery tools are not fine enough for porcelain. Scalpels with interchangeable blades of extreme sharpness are especially useful for carving and piercing porcelain, and so are small-bladed craft knives, as these are finer and sharper than the regular potter's knife and are designed for intricate and delicate work. You can buy these knives in most art shops. Alternatively, you can make your own tools relatively easily and cheaply from discarded hacksaw blades, packing-case binding, clock springs or wire. Grind them on a grindstone to make blades or loops of just the right size and shape.

CARVING, COMBING AND SCRATCHING

The techniques of carving, combing and scratching can produce some of the most beautiful decorative effects on porcelain, especially when they are combined with fluid glazes. The decoration may be shallow or deep and of linear or three-dimensional design, covering all or part of the work.

Combining these techniques can create decorative work of great complexity, taking many hours to achieve, or you can use them simply and directly to decorate a form or to draw attention to a particular part of the pot, such as the rim. You can also use carving to change the line of a rim or foot.

It is very easy to go too far with pierced and carved work, and either make a hole in it or break a piece off. You can sometimes

Margaret O'Rorke A selection of tools used to carve porcelain: some are made from clock springs or wire

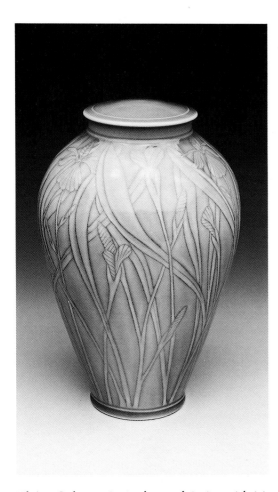

Elaine Coleman Incised porcelain jar with iris decoration. Blue-green celadon glaze, 35.5 × 20 cm (14 × 8 in)

mend a break by replacing the broken part, using stiff porcelain dampened with vinegar, or, if the broken piece is not too damaged, by scoring and joining it in place with vinegar slip.

The marks from carving and piercing often have slight burrs on the edges, but removing them with a damp sponge will take away the detail. Fine steel wool or a soft toothbrush are more effective when used on hard but not dry clay. These still make fine dust, however, so you must wear a face-mask and collect the dust carefully, either by extraction or very regular cleaning.

IMPRESSING

Being so fine and smooth, porcelain is able to take on the most delicate impressed detail, which is somehow 'tightened' through the process of firing. In this way, it is unlike many stoneware clays, where the more textured surface interferes with very fine detail. You can impress porcelain with almost anything, from found objects of natural origin, such as shells, to industrially-made items such as screws or plastic toys. You can also use purpose-made stamps of biscuited porcelain, which are more durable than plaster of Paris and are easier to carve as leather-hard clay. For all-over impressed decoration on porcelain slabs, you can use a textured rolling pin, or roll porcelain on to a textured surface such as textured wall or floor covering.

INLAYING

Coloured porcelain slip can be inlayed into hand-built or thrown porcelain to make crisp and durable designs at the surface level. Inlay is often characterized by the linear or 'drawn' qualities of the marks, and these work well with the white background of the porcelain, echoing the reference to drawing on paper.

Scratch, carve or impress your design for inlaying into the porcelain, and then over-fill it with stained porcelain slip to form a slight bulge, as the slip will shrink considerably as it dries. (A small amount of a deflocculant added to the stained slip will help to keep it fluid and minimize shrinkage.) You can apply slip with a slip trailer or a soft brush. Using a stippling action will prevent the trapping of air bubbles in the grooves, which will show up as holes when you scrape the slip level with the surface. This should be done when the work has become very leather-hard, to reveal the design.

Wrap the freshly slipped work in polythene so that the dampness of the body and slip can equalize. This is important with porcelain because of its high shrinkage rate; if you scrape the inlay level before the two have equalized, the inlay is likely to continue shrinking and to crack. Removing the slip when the work is too damp will also smudge and soften the lines. (You can take away any minor flaws or smudges using wet-and-dry sandpaper after the biscuit firing.) You can turn thrown pots which have been inlaid, but the tools tend to remove too much clay and the design can quickly be lost. Flexible metal kidneys make useful turning tools, as they take away just a little clay at a time.

SPRIGGING

Sprig moulds can be used to make repeatable, raised decoration which is applied to the surface of the work. The 'sprigs' are usually small-scale and of a depth that does not require hollowing. Press plastic porcelain firmly into the mould, and scrape it level with a kidney or knife to make a sprig. This should release easily but, once you have used the mould a few times and it has become damp, you will only be able to lift out the sprig by pressing a small plug of porcelain on to it. As you make the sprigs, store them in polythene to keep them moist; porcelain on this small scale dries very quickly. You can join the sprigs to the form using slip and scoring when you have made a sufficient number.

FLUTING

Fluting has been used for centuries as a means of decorating forms simply and elegantly with a linear design. The flutes often run vertically up the pot, or nearly so, as this seems the most natural direction of the hand and tool when working rythmically and confidently. With time, practice and dexterity, you will be able to make complex curvilinear

patterns, although these might also be described as carving.

The potter Chris Staley uses a wire to cut his thrown pots into a complex series of facets, rather than flutes, when the work is still soft from the throwing, whereas David Leach flutes his porcelain teapots with a bamboo tool when they are leather-hard. Bamboo is one of the hardest woods and makes excellent pottery tools; bamboo fluting tools are available from pottery suppliers (see pages 110–11) or, alternatively, you can grind flat metal blades at an angle to make fluting tools of suitable width.

PORCELAIN SLIPS

Coloured porcelain slips can be painted, sponged, trailed, sprayed and inlaid on to porcelain, as with other clays. Raw porcelain very quickly becomes wet and prone to collapse, however, so the slips must be applied with more care than on other clays. The purity and whiteness of porcelain mean that the colours of porcelain slips are very bright and true: as when painting on a sheet of white paper, the colours are unaffected by the background, and can range in tone from very light to dark. With the exception of true reds, you can make almost any colour using the wide range of body stains currently

Chris Staley *Faceted, salt-fired vase. Height 69 cm (27 in)*

available. Although they provide good colour, slips tend to be opaque by nature, especially when they are heavily stained or thick, and so using slip can obscure the translucency of the porcelain.

Coloured porcelain slips (and bodies) are very effective if left unglazed. Their surfaces are durable and pleasing to touch, the decoration remains crisp, and the matt colours have a particular appeal. Porcelain slips can of course be glazed, but it is often difficult to find a suitable glaze with just the right degree of transparency and brilliance, and which does not cause the colours in the slips to bleed. Soft, slightly matt translucent glazes tend to tone down the colours of the slips but complement the porcelain.

DECORATIVE RESISTS

Resists of wax, paper, latex and adhesive tapes of different widths can be used with slips, oxides and underglaze colours on porcelain, as with other clays. Resists are particularly effective on porcelain when they create layers of translucence. This is achieved by applying a resist to the raw porcelain, and then gradually washing away the body with a sponge, making the wall thinner so that more light will pass through the washed area when it is fired. Use a natural sponge for the washing, as this will leave fewer marks than a synthetic sponge, and will be less likely to abraid the resist. You must carry out the process slowly and gradually, or the pot will

Caroline Whyman *Porcelain lamp with decoration created using wax resist and then washing away the porcelain background. Height 30 cm (12 in). Photograph by Colin Hawkins*

collapse from too much wetting. You can add successive layers of resist, and wash away more porcelain, to make complex patterns and to add greater variety in the translucence.

Shellac is a useful resist for this technique. Painted on the surface of the porcelain, it is waterproof when dry but burns away in the kiln. Shellac is sold through good hardware stores, as well as paint and varnish merchants. It is often viscous and can be thinned with methylated spirit, which is also used for cleaning the brushes.

BISCUIT PORCELAIN

Oxides and underglaze colours are usually associated with the decoration of biscuited porcelain but you can also carve biscuited porcelain, using very sharp tools, although the marks will be less fluid than on leather-hard porcelain. You can use slips and engobes on biscuited porcelain, and these will be easier to apply if you dampen the biscuit pot with water first.

Inke and Uwe Lerch-Brodersen decorate biscuit porcelain with a slip made from their porcelain body coloured with oxides. They apply the slips thinly, so that they do not peel off in the glaze firing. If your porcelain slip does craze or peel, you should lower the

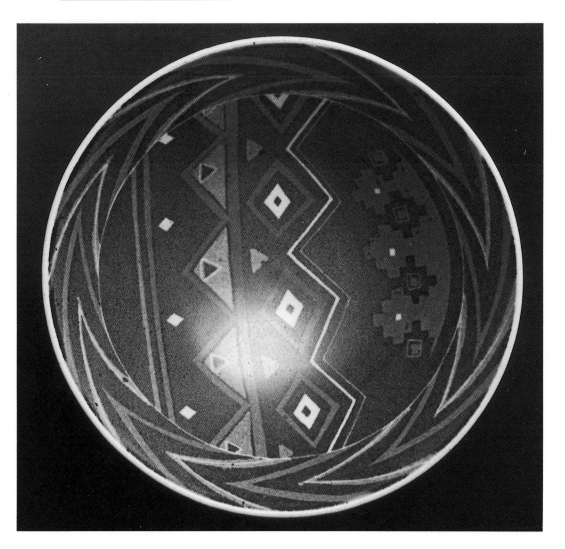

Sheila Casson ‘*Oriental Carpet*’ *porcelain bowl. 20 cm (8 in) diameter. Photograph by John Coles*

plastic-clay content and replace some, or even all, of the China clay with calcined China clay. You can also add a flux such as nephaline syenite or potash feldspar. Although it is much less usual to apply slips to biscuited porcelain than to greenware, it certainly makes handling and applying decoration on delicate forms much less hazardous.

Sheila Casson: vitreous slip for biscuit

Feldspar	60
China clay	40
Cobalt or other oxide	as required

UNDERGLAZE COLOURS AND OXIDES

A glance through pottery suppliers' catalogues will reveal a plethora of colours – both powdered and ready-mixed – for use under the glaze, on top of the raw glaze or over the fired glaze (lustres or enamels). These materials can be applied by sponging, brushing, spraying, masking, or with wax or latex resist. Painting with a proprietary medium will help to bind powdery colours to the surface, but mixing them with water is easier, provided that you handle the work carefully.

Although underglaze painting is usually applied to biscuited porcelain, painting on to leather-hard clay has advantages. The surface is less porous, allowing the brush to flow freely, and you can scratch the painted mark decoratively to show the porcelain beneath. You can also carefully scrape off mistakes! You must handle the painted greenware carefully for packing and glazing, or it will smudge. I have heard of potters using hairspray to seal the colours on to raw ware so that it is easier to pack!

Cobalt and other oxides are still very popular for decorating porcelain. Everyone is familiar with the traditional 'blue-and-white' painting, and there are many different shades and hues of this blue. Today, cobalt is chemically very pure, and – used on its own – gives a hard, strident blue, whereas the cobalt of the past was an impure substance whose contaminants modified and softened the blues, making them more subtle. It is not uncommon now for cobalt to be modified by as many as seven different ingredients, which may make up 80 per cent of the pigment. The usual oxides used to modify cobalt are manganese, iron oxide in its various forms, nickel, rutile, China clay, red clay and talc. Bernard Leach in *A Potter's Book* (see the Bibliography on page 109) recommends a mixture of 98 per cent raw ochre to 2 per cent cobalt oxide, while Derek Emms uses 92 per cent red clay, 4 per cent cobalt carbonate and 4 per cent manganese dioxide.

Adding China clay will help to stick the cobalt mix to the biscuit, and small amounts of Cornish stone ground with the cobalt will make a thin, pale wash of blue that is difficult to achieve with pure cobalt, and which you can then over-paint with darker detail.

Derek Clarkson: blue-grey (for painting on unfired glaze)

Cobalt carbonate	8
Red iron oxide	3.5
China clay	0.5

Unless you intend to use the speckling of cobalt in these mixtures to aesthetic advantage you will need to mix the ingredients carefully, either by sieving them through a fine 200-mesh sieve or by grinding, using a pestle and mortar or a palette knife on a glazed tile. In Japan, the national beverage of green tea is used as a medium with which to paint cobalt on to biscuited porcelain.

It takes time to develop decorating skills, especially hand-painting. Each brush has its own character, so you should familiarize yourself with the kind of marks that each makes. Some brushes leave soft marks while others produce chiselled forms, and some, with very long hairs, are designed to carry a large amount of colour for banding lines on pots without running out of colour. Getting to know each brush before decorating a pot is helpful; try forming lines, zig-zags and simple letterforms, allowing the brush to 'dance' over the surface to find its natural inclination. Try combining several of these forms to create a pattern, composed of various layers

Caroline Whyman Underglaze-blue painting on raw porcelain. The edge of the decoration and the rim are resisted with coloured latex. A pale underglaze blue is painted on using a chisel-ended brush

A smaller chisel-ended brush with a thicker application of underglaze blue is used to outline the first mark

A cotton bud is used to fill the spaces between the brushmarks with spots of underglaze blue

A round-ended brush creates a soft, freely painted line to complete the outline of the original shapes

The tip of the large chisel-ended brush is dabbed to make parallel lines. (The latex is peeled off before the biscuit firing)

A round-ended metal tool is used to scratch through the painted decoration in order to reveal the raw porcelain beneath

and tones, or try placing shapes against one another (see illustrations). The cheap paper sold as lining paper for walls is a good surface on which to practise brushmarks.

You can also paint oxides and commercial colours on to the freshly applied glaze, and scratch or scrape them to alter the marks, which will soften as the glaze melts in the kiln. Most oxides and stains are strong and should be applied fairly thinly, like watercolours, although some oxides when applied thickly can produce interesting colour effects and may cause runs. These runs may be decorative, but will be difficult to control.

ENAMELS AND LUSTRES

Enamels (or onglaze, as they are also known) and lustres provide an unusual and very broad palette of colours for decorating porcelain. They should be applied to porcelain after it has been high-fired, either on the glaze or directly on to the fired clay.

ENAMELS
Enamels can be painted in great detail, and, when fired well, do not blend or blush into one another, so that they enhance the porcelain with their bright colours. True reds, oranges, and pinks – which are difficult or impossible to achieve at the top temperatures – are attainable with enamels. However, enamel painting must be handled carefully if it is not to appear garish and cheap. Enamel decoration should be fired to between 750–

850°C (1382–1562°F) so that the colours are just bonded on to the surface of the glaze, and, at their best, appear jewel-like in their brilliance.

You can buy enamels ready-mixed, for application with water or medium, or as powders for mixing with fat oil to the correct consistency before you apply them (see the List of Suppliers on pages 110–11).

LUSTRES
Lustres can range from rich and opulent golds and platinums, through a wide range of iridescent colours, to subtle mother-of-pearls. Their surfaces reflect the glaze or body qualities beneath them: matt on matt surfaces, and brilliantly glassy on shiny surfaces. Lustres are fired slightly lower than enamels, to between 650–780°C (1202–1436°F).

When painting lustres, it is vital that you keep separate brushes for the precious metals, golds and platinums and do not use them to paint other lustres, in order to prevent contamination which will change the colours. You should also keep the brushes and any mixing palettes clean and free from dust; you can clean them with pure turpentine, lustre thinners or essence. I keep two containers of turpentine for each set of brushes; one for the first wash, which quickly becomes dirty, and the second, which is kept cleaner, for the final wash. A plentiful supply of lint-free rags is also useful for cleaning brushes.

Apply lustres thinly as they will burn out if

you apply them too thickly. For more information on lustres, see *The Complete Potter: Lustres* by Margery Clinton (see the Bibliography on page 109).

COLOURED PORCELAIN BODIES

Introducing colour and pattern as an integral part of the forming process, by using stained porcelain clay, can produce very successful results, in which smoothness and strength are combined with strong colours and the ability to create super-fine detail. There are many different ways of patterning the stained porcelain, including agate, *neriage*, *nerikomi*, lamination, as well as inlaying and marquetry. Each method of combining the coloured porcelains has its own particular quality.

AGATE
The naturally occurring patterns achieved by loosely wedging and kneading stained bodies together are known as agate, and have a similarity to geological formations or the patterns of oil on water. The loosely wedged clay can be thrown, coiled, slabbed or moulded.

NERIAGE
The technique of throwing coloured clays is known as *neriage* in Japan. The longer and more complex the throwing process, the more

Thomas Hoadley *Nerikomi bowl, stained*
porcelain 11.5 × 20 × 21.5 cm (4½ × 8 × 8½in)

intermixed the colours become, thinning and spiralling their way around the form. The thrown surface becomes 'muddied' from the intermixing of the colours, and the true pattern is only revealed when the pot is turned on both sides.

NERIKOMI

The Japanese term *nerikomi* is given to coloured clays which have been *systematically* wedged together, sliced and re-assembled, and then hand-formed, often involving the use of moulds. This technique is used with dexterity and patience by potter Thomas Hoadley (see photograph, page 61). He describes his work in the following way: 'Coloured clays are sliced and stacked repeatedly to form patterns and colour/textures in the clay itself, resulting in a single block or loaf made up of thousands of overlapping layers. Cross-sectional slices are cut from the block and joined together to form vessels. The many layers are thus revealed as fine undulating lines imbedded in a surrounding colour. The pattern becomes the substance and the structure of the form itself, rather than just a surface embellishment.'

The slices cut from the block are joined and formed in press moulds, or used more freely in conjunction with a leather-hard base to form gently undulating walls. The process of joining the slices of coloured porcelain inevitably smudges the surface, but this can be cleaned up with a metal kidney when the

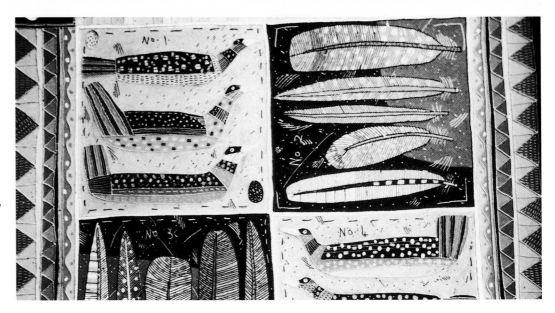

work is leather-hard. The surfaces can be refined further by wet-sanding after both firings to give a very smooth, silky finish.

LAMINATION

With laminated porcelain, an even more controlled pattern is possible. The technique involves rolling sheets of coloured porcelain, which are cut and then rejoined with slip. This new sheet of clay is then repeatedly rolled, cut and trimmed in increasingly complex combinations, to form either a block or a sheet of patterned clay. This procedure may be repeated many times with different colour combinations and patterns. The process may be interrupted at any time, and extra sheets or coils of a contrasting colour can be added and rolled repeatedly. This has

Joanna Veevers Detail of 'Ducks and Feathers' panel. 21 × 21 cm (8¼ × 8¼in)

the effect of shrinking the design, making a clay *millefiore*. The finely patterned slabs and coils are cut and joined in patterns in a hollow mould.

Sue Nemeth uses coloured porcelain in a very direct way to create collages (see pages 92–3). Joanna Veevers (see above) makes her graphically decorated porcelain murals as tiles on a slab of plaster, which she engraves with a design and then paints with coloured porcelain slips. She picks up the image from the plaster by casting over the painted design with slip, which is retained by a wall of clay, forming the body of the tile.

CHAPTER SEVEN

COLOUR, GLAZES AND GLAZING

Porcelain is fired to a high temperature and the composition of the body is similar to the glaze, so that the integration between the body and the glaze is almost complete. As a result, glazed porcelain has a special quality which is closer to semi-precious stones than to fired earth, especially if the body is translucent. Unlike iron-bearing clays, where the body influences the colour response, porcelain provides a neutral ground which reflects the true colour of glazes and stains.

The range of colour that can be achieved with porcelain is as wide as the ceramic palette can offer, from the palest of hues to the brilliant, strong colours of glazes and enamels, including some of the most elusive but rewarding glazes, such as the chuns and copper-reds. In addition, while white earthenware may also be glazed and decorated with brilliant colours, its fired

Colin Pearson Porcelain jug with convolute handle. Height 37.5 cm (15 in)

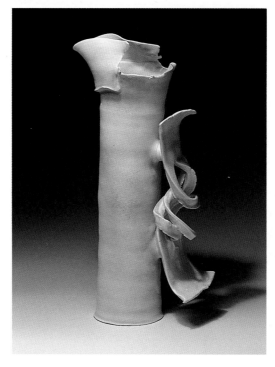

qualities are not the same as those of porcelain. Earthenware glazes form a distinct layer that is separate from the body, which sometimes gives the colours more of the qualities of paint than glaze.

COLOUR IN SLIPS AND BODIES

For consistent and speckle-free results, you will find it easier to prepare coloured porcelain slips and bodies with dry porcelain, such as trimmings from turning, because you can weigh the porcelain accurately and add the correct percentage of stain. Powdered porcelain from pottery suppliers is not always suitable for making coloured bodies or slips, as it is often formulated for casting and lacks bentonite, which makes the body short and brittle. You can overcome this by adding 1–2 per cent of macalloid or bentonite.

It is possible to add most stains to porcelain in larger quantities than the

guidelines given by manufacturers, and some potters use up to 20 per cent of body stains in order to achieve an intense colour. However, the darker stains, such as the blues and black, and most oxides, are not suitable in high saturations because they begin to act as a flux, making the surface glossy or causing the body to bloat and slump. You should test stained bodies in small quantities before mixing them in large amounts.

For colours to be completely integrated into the porcelain, you will need to soak the dry ingredients overnight with hot water before mixing them and screening them through a 100-mesh sieve. A hand-held food blender will cut down the time that you spend in mixing small quantities of coloured slips, and in reconstituting thickened slips. You can make coloured bodies from slips by drying them on plaster batts – discarded press moulds are even better, as they hold the slip and prevent it from flowing into a thin pancake. A fine, clean, cotton cloth placed between the slip and the plaster will facilitate the removal of the coloured porcelain while preventing the plaster from undue staining.

You can mix powdered stains and oxides directly into plastic porcelain, but this process is more difficult and time-consuming, especially if you intend the results to be

Geoffrey Eastop *Wide, grogged-porcelain pot, painted with black, orange and grey vitreous slips. Height 30.5 cm (12 in)*

speckle-free. Mix the stain or oxide to a paste with hot water and spread it on to thin slices of porcelain, and then stack these before wedging and kneading them thoroughly. Alternatively, you can put the paste into a roughly shaped bowl of plastic porcelain, and repeatedly fold and knead it. With either method, you should keep a record of the proportions and colours that you have used, and fire a test button as a colour guide. You can intermix most coloured bodies to make a wide range of colours, and lighten them by adding unstained porcelain.

DECORATION

Coloured porcelain bodies, extruded to a suitable length and thickness through a hand extruder, make ceramic crayons or pencils for decoration. Adding between 0.25 and 0.5 per cent of sodium silicate to the ingredients will strengthen some colours and reduce the amount of water that you need for mixing. Fire the pencils to between 800–900°C (1472–1652°F); lower firing will make a softer crayon.

You can make wax crayons by mixing liquid wax with the dry ingredients, without the deflocculant, and then air-drying them after they have been extruded. Most art shops sell holders which are suitable for the fired crayons.

Caroline Whyman *Thrown and impressed porcelain teapot. Height 17 cm (6¾in)*

PORCELAIN GLAZES

Porcelain glazes can be divided into two broad groups: those which are transparent, or nearly so, and show to advantage any decoration beneath the glaze; and those which are opaque and generally silky or matt, and often have a tactile, sensuous surface.

The recipes for and ingredients of many porcelain glazes are similar to those of porcelain bodies, but specify increased amounts of flux and contain only a handful of different materials. The earliest Chinese glazes were made from as little as two or three ingredients: the simplest, which is still used today, was a combination of calcined

limestone and feldspar, in the form of petunse.

There are many published recipes for stoneware and porcelain glazes which make a starting point for developing glazes, especially for those potters whose approach is empirical and practical, and who are not greatly interested in the theory and formulae for glaze calculation. However, one person's successful glaze formula can be very different when mixed and fired by someone else, because there are so many variables: fuel, temperature, firing cycle, body, thickness of glaze and method of application, as well as the variability of materials which have come from different sources.

Whatever your approach to making glazes, knowing something about the properties of the various materials will help to inform your choice. In simple terms, a glaze is composed of silica, alumina and flux. The silica, which makes up the bulk of the glaze, is the glass-former, while alumina, often in the form of clay, acts as a stiffener. The flux reduces the melting point of the silica. High-fired glazes are often referred to as 'lime glazes', 'feldspathic glazes', 'dolomite glazes', 'barium matt glazes', etc., and these descriptions refer to the dominant flux in the glaze and its characteristics.

SILICA

Quartz and flint are both silica. They are the chief glass-formers, and give hardness and durability to the glaze when used in amounts of up to 20 per cent with a fine (200- or 300-) mesh size. Larger amounts of quartz and flint increase the maturing temperature of the glaze, while lower amounts give a glassier melt but increase the tendency to craze. In Nigel Wood's book, *Oriental Glazes* (see the Bibliography on page 109), he recommends the limits for silica given below:

Cone 7 1230°C (2246°F) silica		67
Cone 8 1250°C (2282°F) silica		68
Cone 9 1280°C (2336°F) silica		69
Cone 10 1300°C (2372°F) silica		70–1

Alumina

The main source of alumina in glazes is the clays, and they also supply some silica. Clay aids the suspension of the glaze, and increases its unfired strength. It increases the viscosity of the molten glaze, preventing it from running, while large quantities of clay opacify the glaze.

China clay is used in porcelain glazes for its purity, but it shrinks and can cause crawling, especially in thicker glazes. However, calcined China clay can be substituted for amounts of over 10 per cent and shrinks to a lesser extent. Pure ball clays can be used in small amounts, but shrink even more than China clay. Bentonite in an amount of between 1–3 per cent is very useful for suspending glazes and for increasing the strength of unfired glaze, especially in recipes with little or no clay content.

FLUX

The fluxes, which lower the melting point of the silica and alumina and give the glaze its character, are various. The first five materials in the following list are the primary fluxes for porcelain glazes, and the additional fluxes are often used with these. The additional fluxes are often referred to as 'secondary fluxes', and may also be used in combination with each other or on their own.

Whiting or lime

This is the principal flux in many porcelain glazes, and contains calcium carbonate. Lime glazes are characterized by their hard, durable, glassy surfaces. At 15–25 per cent, however, lime can act as an anti-flux and dull the glaze, which can be attractive. In the larger amounts, lime makes the glazes matt with a micro-crystalline surface.

Soda and potash feldspars

These form the other principal high-temperature fluxes, along with whiting. Like clay, feldspars contain alumina and silica, but also include a higher proportion of the fluxes sodium and potassium. Potash feldspar is a natural frit, forming a stiff, glassy melt at around 1250°C (2282°F).

As it forms a glaze on its own, potash feldspar is a useful ingredient in porcelain glazes, needing only 5–10 per cent of secondary flux, with a little clay and flint, to make a workable glaze. Although it generally forms 50 per cent of a glaze, potash feldspar

*Caroline **Whyman** 'Sun and Moon'.
Thrown porcelain bowl.
Crackle glaze with a stained
triangle and circle design,
35.5 cm (14 in) diameter*

in amounts of up to 85 per cent will produce a milky or semi-opaque glaze, but this will have a tendency to craze. Soda feldspar is similar to potash feldspar, but fuses at a lower temperature, and is less commonly used.

Cornish stone or Carolina stone

This is very similar in composition and behaviour to the feldspars, but it contains more silica and so has a higher melting point. Calcium, magnesium, fluorine, iron and titanium may be present as trace elements. A very simple and reliable glaze can be made from 85:15 Cornish stone to whiting. I have used this combination as a basis for a transparent porcelain glaze with a subtle sheen (rather than a bright gloss), which crackles attractively.

Caroline Whyman: large-crackle glaze (Cone 8)

Cornish stone	82
Nepheline syenite	4
Whiting	12
Borocalcite frit	2
Calcined China clay	4
Bentonite	2

In this recipe, the nepheline syenite and frit lower the firing temperature, making the glaze more fluid, while the bentonite and clay help to suspend the ingredients and to increase the dry strength of this otherwise powdery glaze. The glaze must be applied thickly, and it is easiest to do this by spraying. The crackle may be enhanced by staining it with waterproof drawing ink after firing.

Nepheline syenite

This is a useful flux that gives bright, clear glazes, although the glazes are prone to crazing. It melts at a lower temperature than feldspar or Cornish stone and can be substituted for part or all of these two fluxes in order to lower the firing temperature of a glaze.

Colin Pearson: glaze with restrained gloss (Cone 7–8 oxidation)

Nepheline syenite	40.3
Lithium carbonate	4.3
Whiting	8.7
Quartz	46.6
Bentonite	2

Wood ash

This acts as a very powerful flux. It forms a glaze simply by being heated in contact with the clay body, either as 'fly ash' from wood fuel, or by deliberate application in a glaze or on its own. Wood ash contains a high proportion of the alkali fluxes of sodium, potassium and calcium. Some are soluble in water and must be handled with caution, as they can irritate the skin – wear rubber gloves for mixing, washing ash or sieving. Wood ash is also made up of silica, alumina and small quantities of other materials, which make ash an exciting if unpredictable material.

Glazes containing ash are characterized by a broken-textured surface. They are inclined to run, so they should be used with great care on porcelain or the result may appear messy. Rutile with other oxides in ash glaze can produce soft, mottled colours. For very simple ash glazes, use equal parts of wood ash, feldspar and clay, or 2 parts wood ash and 1 part clay. Derek Davis uses 2 parts beech ash and 2 parts feldspar with 1 part China clay for an ash glaze that matures at 1300°C (2372°F).

Dolomite

This is made up of calcium and magnesium in equal parts. Using dolomite in amounts of up to 20 per cent will make a smooth, buttery, dense glaze with pleasant tactile qualities. With cobalt (less than 2 per cent), high-dolomite glazes may be lilac or purple rather than blue, and with copper in oxidation they can be grey or browny-pink rather than green.

Talc

This consists of magnesium and silica and can give similar effects to dolomite, although it is a less powerful flux. Unlike dolomite, talc tends to inhibit crazing.

*Right: **Uwe Lerch** Thrown porcelain vase with dolomite glaze. 17 × 20 cm (6½ × 8 in)*

Jack Doherty: soft, satiny glaze (Cone 10 reduction)

Talc	23
Nepheline syenite	20
China clay	22
Whiting	13
Flint	22

Magnesium carbonate

This tends to make glazes smooth and silky, and is generally used in quantities of less than 10 per cent. Even small quantities of this flux can make glazes extremely dry.

Sheila Casson: green magnesium glaze (1280–1300°C [2372°F] reduction)

Cornish stone	33
Whiting	7
Ball clay	4
Magnesium carbonate	2
China clay	6
Iron oxide	1.5–3

Barium carbonate

This is a toxic material, and must be handled with caution. In glazes it is used in amounts from 10–50 per cent, and typically produces either a satin-matt surface, or, in large quantities, fires to a very dry and textured surface. Used with copper carbonate or oxide, barium carbonate has a high alkaline response, producing brilliant blues and turquoises. If you add boric oxide, in the form of colemanite, gerstly borate or borocalcite frit, to barium glazes, the melt will be more fluid and the surface less matt.

Delan Cookson '*Tulip Vase*'.
Thrown and assembled porcelain
vase with barium glaze,
height 20 cm (8 in)

Delan Cookson: blue glaze (Cone 8 oxidation)

Nepheline syenite	40
Barium carbonate	35
Whiting	5
Lithium carbonate	3
China clay	10
Flint	7
Copper carbonate	2

Colemanite

This is a powerful flux containing boron and calcium. It has a bright colour response, and is useful for adding texture to a glaze. In transparent glazes, colemanite gives a milky-blue opalescence where thick. However, many potters find colemanite a difficult ingredient to use, as it causes the glaze to 'spit off' on to the kiln shelves, or to crawl. Gerstly borate or borocalcite frit can act as substitutes.

Lithium carbonate

This is a highly active flux (as I discovered to my cost when I mistook it for placing powder – it corroded and melted the bricks in the base of my kiln to a depth of 6 cm (2½ in) in a single firing!) Used in small quantities (often less than 4 per cent) as a secondary flux, lithium carbonate gives beautiful alkaline glazes with a semi-matt, very fine crystalline surface; for example, copper becomes turquoise rather than green. Lithium carbonate is useful in porcelain glazes because of its low expansion; this decreases the tendency of the glaze to craze.

Petalite

This is a flux with similar melting properties to feldspar, but containing lithium. As a result, petalite, unlike feldspar, has a slightly alkaline colour response. Petalite is a useful substitute for nephaline syenite in porcelain glazes because of its very low thermal expansion.

Bone ash

This contains phosphorous and calcium, and is made from calcined bones. Using bone ash in amounts of between 0.5 to 10 per cent can produce opalescence in glazes. Bone ash has a tendency to trap minute air bubbles in glaze, which do not clear when 'soaked', and can be opacifying in effect. Many chun glazes contain phosphorous.

Titanium dioxide

Although not strictly a flux, this can have a significant effect on the quality of a glaze in amounts as little as 0.2 per cent. In his book *Oriental Glazes* (see the Bibliography on page 109), Nigel Wood says: 'More than 0.1 per cent of titanium will make the glaze (iron-bearing reduced celadon) fire more green than blue.' As little as 2 per cent acts as an opacifier and, because of its extreme refactoriness, titanium dioxide makes glazes dry and matt. It is a useful modifier of colours: for example, titanium and cobalt react together to give soft greens.

Zinc oxide

This acts in a similar way to titanium. Small amounts of 2–3 per cent produce strong fluxing effects, lowering the maturing temperature of the glaze, while quantities of approximately 8 per cent can cause the glaze surface to become dry and sugary, and often prone to pinholing and pitting. It can also result in a dull colour response with some oxides. However, zinc oxide can help prevent crazing: as little as 0.3 per cent discourages settling and sedimentation in lithium glazes.

Delan Cookson: red/green glaze (Cone 8 oxidation)

Potash feldspar	65
China clay	6
Flint	34
Zinc oxide	40
Barium carbonate	60
Lithium carbonate	7
Nickel oxide (black)	8

COLOUR IN GLAZES

Colour in porcelain glazes is created using oxides and stains. It is dependent on the kiln atmosphere – either reducing or oxidizing – and on the fluxes in the glaze: for example, copper will yield a turquoise colour only in an alkaline glaze. The two most versatile oxides for their wide range of colour response must be iron and copper. Large amounts of iron in high-firing glazes may give rich tenmokus of black or dark brown, some with rich rust edges or speckles. Smaller amounts of iron will cause glazes to fire from browns to honeys in oxidation, and very small amounts of iron in reduction make wonderful celadon blues and greens. As well as giving green in oxidation, copper can also produce blues, turquoises and salmony pinks, but in reduction the copper-reds appear, ranging from a bright red through 'ox-blood' to aubergine, lilac and pale pink.

Derek Clarkson: copper-red glaze (1280–1300°C [2336–2372°F] reduction)

Soda feldspar	27
Flint	12
Whiting	9
China clay	3
Standard alkaline frit	9
Tin oxide	3
Copper carbonate	1

Derek Emms: celadon glaze (1280°C [2336°F] reduction) (*Ceramic Review*, issue no. 124, 1990)

China clay	10
Wollastonite	20
Flint	30
Feldspar (water-ground)	40
Talc	5
Molochite	5
Zinc oxide	5
Red iron oxide (synthetic)	0.5

Note: Ball mill for four hours.

Cobalt, which is often used with porcelain, gives a deep strong blue whether reduced or oxidized, but it can be modified with other oxides, such as iron, manganese and nickel, to tone down the blue. For more information on colour in glaze, see the Bibliography on page 109 (*The Ceramic Spectrum* by Robin Hopper is useful for indicating the range of colour response).

Adding commercial body and glaze stains to transparent glazes will produce a wide variety of colours and tones on porcelain. In order to achieve the best colour results with commercial stains, use a base glaze that is high in lime, and contains no zinc oxide, which can make the colours dull or dirty. To avoid speckles, soak the stains with the glaze ingredients overnight before mixing or sieving them, and blunge where possible.

GLAZE MIXING AND APPLICATION

You should mix porcelain glazes in much the same way as other glazes, by paying attention to weighing ingredients accurately. Keep dust to a minimum, and wear a face-mask. As there is a problem with crazing in many porcelain glazes, you should sieve the ingredients through a fine sieve (100 mesh) to integrate the particles more completely. It is even better if you can ball-mill the glaze to help prevent crazing. Milling also gives a much better glaze melt, often at a lower temperature.

Although you can glaze porcelain using the normal methods, the biscuit is often thin in section, so you must plan the glazing carefully in order to allow the water from the glaze to dry out. A good method is to glaze the inside and outside separately so that the glaze can dry, or to force-dry the glazed work with anything from a hairdrier to an electric paint-stripper.

SPRAYING

Many potters, because of the problem of glazing fine porcelain, spray their glazes on for a smooth, drip-free surface, which suits the often flawless quality of the porcelain body. You can control variations in colour and texture by spraying the glaze in different thicknesses, and build up complex patterns by spraying over masks made of paper or latex. You must use a specially designed spray booth or an enclosed area that is adequately vented to collect the spray dust, and wear a tight-fitting face-mask to prevent the inhalation of glaze particles. Spraying has the advantage of requiring only small amounts of glaze, and, although some is lost during spraying, it can be scraped off and saved. This is inadvisable with transparent glaze if you are spraying coloured glazes in the same booth, however, as it is very difficult to avoid contamination.

DIPPING AND POURING

If you have no spray equipment, dipping and pouring are the preferred alternatives for glazing, although you will need larger quantities of glaze. With practice, you will find it possible to glaze quickly, with an even coating. In order to prevent a double layer of glaze from forming on your work, carefully paint a layer of wax over the first application of glaze where necessary.

BRUSHING

Some glazes are suitable for brushing on to porcelain, but you will only be able to achieve smooth surfaces with very fluid glazes, such as crystal glazes, which are usually brushed on thickly at the top of the pot and more thinly towards the base. When applying glazes with a brush, add 0.5 per cent glaze binder or CMC gum. This will help the

Peter Lane 'Confetti'. *Thrown porcelain bowl with air-brushed and resist design, 15 × 18.5 cm (6 × 7¼in)*

layers of glaze to bond to the biscuit, and will increase the handling qualities of the work for kiln packing.

COMBINING GLAZES

Applying two different glazes on top of one other provides decorative possibilities. You can try double-dipping, trailing, scratching, resisting with wax or even inlaying the glazes, using a sharp scalpel to cut away the base glaze. Some combinations will react with surprising results, but the overall application must not be too thick or the combined glazes will be likely to run.

GLAZE AND BODY FAULTS

One potter's glaze fault can be another potter's artistic effect. You should be careful in your judgements on the merits and aesthetics of such glazes, as the industrial ideals of smoothness and perfection – while they have their attraction in association with porcelain – are by no means the only aesthetic. Crystalline matts, lava glazes and the dry, bright qualities of some alkaline glazes, all of which have a wide range of tactile and visual excitement to contribute to porcelain glazing, were developed in recent years as departures from traditional porcelain glazes. Having said this, there are some surfaces and effects which are unacceptable and can be termed faults.

CRAWLING

Many glaze faults on porcelain stem from problems which occur after the biscuit firing. Some of these are caused by dust and by grease from fingers and hands, which prevent the smooth melting of the glaze, causing it to crawl away from the surface leaving bare areas. Dusting or sponging the biscuited porcelain carefully will help to prevent crawling. Glazes with large amounts of clay or zinc are also liable to crawl. Lowering the amount of zinc and substituting calcined China clay for some of the clay content can overcome this fault.

CRAZING

Another common fault with porcelain glazes is crazing. This effect can be decorative, but it is also an annoying fault that is hard to correct, because porcelain is a low-expansion body (i.e. the glaze shrinks more than the body as it cools after firing, causing it to craze). Achieving a good glaze fit on a porcelain body can require experiment and persistence. Some sources only recommend adding extra silica, but Joanna Howells, who spent some time developing a craze-free glaze, says that a correct glaze fit is ultimately dependent on the ratio of silica to alumina. She found Ian Currie's book *Stoneware Glazes: A Systematic Approach* (see the Bibliography on page 109) very helpful for understanding this fault.

Substituting low-expansion frit or low-expansion equivalent materials can prevent crazing, and China clay with calcined china clay can help. In order to prevent crazing without altering the glaze recipe, however, try ball-milling the glaze for a few hours or overnight.

Joanna Howells: transparent, low-expansion glaze (1270°C [2318°F] reduction)

Potclays low-expansion frit	54
Potash feldspar	16.9
Whiting	14.4
China clay	14.4
Molochite, 200-mesh	5
Silica	10

Derek Emms: low-expansion porcelain glaze (1280°C [2336°F] reduction) (*Ceramic Review*, issue no. 75, 1982)

China clay	15
Molochite, fine	14
Feldspar	25
Quartz	26
Whiting	21

Note: Add red iron oxide (1–2%) for a celadon glaze.

WARPING, BLOATING AND BLISTERING

These faults are mostly attributable to three causes: insufficient clay preparation, over-firing, or inadequate ventilation of the biscuit firing. Firing too quickly or poorly ventilating the biscuit firing causes bloating and blisters, as organic matter in the clay may not be completely burned. Venting the biscuit to the top temperature and either soaking or firing at a rate of not more than 100°C (212°F) per hour can overcome these problems. Poor clay preparation leaves trapped air bubbles in the porcelain, which may reappear as blisters after the glaze firing. The only substitute for thorough wedging and kneading is a de-airing pug mill. For bloating associated with over-firing (for which there is no remedy except to learn by the mistake), take note of any hot spots in the kiln, and fire to a lower temperature the next time.

PINHOLES

Pinholes in porcelain glazes can be unsightly. They often occur when the kiln is under-fired, catching the glaze when it is insufficiently melted to heal over any bubbles. This fault can usually be resolved by firing higher, or by soaking the kiln for a time at the same temperature. However, glazes containing zinc may pinhole but cannot be remedied by soaking, so you must lower the zinc content instead.

STAINING

Unplanned and unsightly staining of the body in reduction-fired porcelain may be caused by incomplete reduction. The body appears creamy where it is oxidized, and grey where it is reduced. This may be the result of insufficient reduction in parts of the kiln, due to the firing cycle or to the position of the pots near the entry of the flame. It can also happen if the reduction begins *after* the glaze has begun to melt, preventing the complete reduction of the body.

Staining may also be caused by 'carbon trap', a fault mostly found in reduction-fired slip-cast porcelain. The causes are not completely understood, but sodium sulphate is thought to be a factor. In his book *Ceramic Faults and their Remedies* (see Bibliography on page 109), Harry Fraser says: 'Sodium sulphate is produced by the reaction (double de-composition) of sodium carbonate and, to a lesser degree, sodium silicate, with the plaster mould (calcium sulphate) ... being commonly used in casting slips as deflocculants.' He recommends the use of an organic deflocculant (such as Dispex, a polyacrylate available from Potclays: see the List of Suppliers on pages 110–11), either on its own or with other deflocculants (except soda ash and silicate), to remedy this.

CHAPTER EIGHT

FIRING AND FINISHING

The packing and firing of porcelain requires greater care than other clays, because porcelain is more fragile to handle as biscuit and greenware, and is likely to warp if overloaded or poorly placed. Cleanliness and order are essential – especially if you use your kiln to fire other clays – as stray spots of oxide, glaze or kiln brick can mar the appearance of porcelain, which almost always demands to be blemish-free.

Before packing any work into the kiln, you must check the shelves carefully for warping, as porcelain will deform to the shape of the shelf. The surfaces of the shelves should be as smooth as possible – you must remove glaze spots, and level uneven layers of batt wash, which build up over time, with a carborundum stone under running water. You should only apply batt wash to one side of the shelf, or flakes can drop off and spoil glazed ware. Batt wash can be brushed on with care, but, for a really smooth finish on new shelves, you can pour it like a thin glaze. Fill areas which have become chipped from the removal of

Thomas Hoadley Nerikomi vase.
$21.5 \times 16.5 \times 14.6\,cm$ ($8\frac{1}{2} \times 6\frac{1}{2} \times 5\frac{3}{4}in$)

glaze spots with kiln cement, scrape this level with the surface of the shelf using a metal scraper or ruler, and then batt wash on top.

PACKING AND FIRING BISCUIT

PREPARING AND PACKING THE KILN

As a precaution before each firing, you should gently vacuum the interior of the kiln to remove any dust or loose brick. You can place the porcelain for biscuit firing in the kiln in contact with other porcelain, but, to avoid cracks or unnecessary stress, most potters stack no more than three pieces on top of each other. You should 'place' smaller work in position to prevent dragging or

Caroline Whyman *Porcelain dish inlaid with dark-blue porcelain slip and gold lustre band and square, diameter 38 cm (15 in)*

pushing the base of the work on the shelves, which will mark the porcelain. Ease larger pieces into position using placing powder or alumina hydrate, which acts like tiny ball bearings to facilitate the movement, and also aids the shrinkage during firing. You can use silica sand in saggars to support unglazed work through both firings.

FIRING

Provided that the work is completely dry and of even thickness, a typical biscuit firing proceeds at 100°C (212°F) per hour until it reaches approximately 650°C (1202°F), when you can turn the kiln to full. For work that is uneven in thickness or slightly damp, however, the firing should be preceded by a very slow warm-up to drive off any water, and a rise of 60–70°C (140–158°F) or slower per hour will be better.

The kiln should be well-ventilated for a biscuit firing, with the bungs out so that all organic matter is burned away. Some potters soak for thirty minutes at the top temperature, in order to ensure complete combustion; this helps to prevent bloating in the glaze firing. I ventilate my biscuit firings to the top temperature of 980°C (1796°F), which gives a soft, porous biscuit, but other potters fire to 1020°C (1868°F). Your preference will depend on your particular kiln and on your method of measuring temperature, as well as on the degree of porosity and strength that you wish to achieve in the biscuit.

You must still handle the work carefully after it is bisqued; delicate areas are all too easy to snap or chip, and your hands must be clean and free of grease, which can prevent the adhesion of the raw glaze. Dust is another problem, causing the glaze to crawl, so you must store any biscuit that is not to be glazed immediately away from dust.

PACKING AND FIRING GLAZE

PACKING THE KILN

The placing and firing of porcelain for glaze firing is critical, and, although some general suggestions can be made, it will only be the experience of using the same kiln and firing schedules that will enable you to place the work for the best results. You will then have discovered the parts of the kiln that are hotter or cooler, and the areas in which the work is more likely to warp, particularly with a flame kiln, where the flow and passage of the flame has an effect on the firing of the work.

In order to minimize warping, avoid placing the work so that it overlaps the edges of shelves, or near the entry ports of the flame. Low or flat work placed on the bottom of the kiln will often under-fire, so pack taller work on the lowest shelf and flatter work in the middle of the kiln. Making a note of the firing details in a kiln log will save you from having to recall the details of previous firings.

PLUCKING

This is a common problem with firing porcelain. It occurs when small pieces of the base or footring of a pot bond on to the kiln shelf during the firing. As the work cools and shrinks, small pieces pull away from the pot in wedge-shaped crescents of razor sharpness, leaving the base of the pot scarred. There are many ways of overcoming this, as well as the related problem of 'ovaling', when the footring catches on the kiln shelf and shrinks unevenly.

For flat bases, you can place alumina hydrate under the work, but, for pots with feet, it is very easy to use too much alumina, bedding the glazed area into the powder which forms an ugly granular mass. Another problem is that any form of placing powder is easy to knock off the shelf during packing, causing it to fall on the work beneath. Some potters use discs of biscuit porcelain coated with alumina or flint to prevent plucking and ovaling on pots with feet, but the discs cannot always be satisfactorily re-used. However, the potter Sheila Casson recommends circles of ceramic-fibre paper for placing porcelain, and says that these can be re-used. Colin Pearson makes flat discs to place his work in the kiln, which he makes from 9 parts alumina and 1 part bentonite. These discs are also re-usable.

LIDS

Porcelain lids are less likely to warp if you fire them in position. However, they do tend

Chris Staley Porcelain soda-fired platter, with slip pulled down. 56 cm (22 in) diameter

to stick to the pot during the firing, which is not surprising as the body is at the point of glassification at high temperatures. Flint mixed with arrowroot (available from grocery stores) is the best way to prevent sticking, but flint must be handled with great care because it is pure silica and must *not* be inhaled. After firing, you should remove the flint *under water* with a fine wire brush, followed by a carborundum stone or wet-and-dry (carborundum) paper, which is a lengthy process. Many potters use alumina hydrate instead of flint, but this is difficult to apply to lids and bases when mixed with water only, and falls off easily when it is dry. Mixing the alumina with wax or glaze binder will make it easier to apply. Alumina is easier than flint to wash off after firing.

OPENING AND UNPACKING THE KILN

The excitement attached to the opening of a glaze firing never seems to dim, even with experience, but with porcelain you must be patient enough to allow the kiln to cool to at least 150°C (302°F) before opening the door. When it is cooled too rapidly, porcelain is prone to 'dunting', which causes the work to crack. This can occur at fairly low temperatures, such as 225°C (437°F), when cristobalite inversion takes place. I have

Sasha Wardell Small and medium stopper vases. Slip-cast bone china, masked and sprayed with ceramic stains. Height 25 and 15 cm (10 and 6 in)

can be silky to touch. You can smooth bases and feet with a carborundum stone or wet-and-dry paper, while lids and galleries are easily smoothed with a valve-grinding paste, available from car-repair shops. Electric grindstones are very quick to use, but are often voracious in their cutting action. A gentle, but fairly speedy, alternative to this method is to hold the base of the pot against a sheet of carborundum paper, which should be stuck on a batt and attached to an electric wheel.

OXIDATION AND REDUCTION FIRING

The choice between firing porcelain in oxidation or reduction is a personal one, and is likely to be dependent on the type of kiln that you have. This is because, while it is possible to reduce in an electric kiln and oxidize in a fuel-burning kiln, the reverse is usually the practice. Another factor is the aesthetic of colour, as both the colour of the body and the colours of many glazes are directly affected and changed by the type of atmosphere in the kiln. Many people acknowledge that reduction firing gives a

learned – through bitter experience – not to open my kiln until the temperature has dropped below 100°C (212°F) especially if I am firing porcelain with a thick crackle glaze. This can literally pull the body apart if it cools too quickly, because the glaze shrinks more than the body.

If you intend to fire lustres over glazed work, be sure to unpack the work from the kiln with clean, dry hands (or, better still, keep a pair of clean cotton gloves for this task), in order to prevent fingermarks from showing after the lustre firing. You should also store the glazed work in a dust-free place. Working in this way should save you from having to de-grease the surface before applying lustre or enamel.

FINISHING
One of the pleasures of handling fired porcelain lies in the smoothness of the body, which, with a little extra work after firing,

Derek Clarkson *Thrown porcelain bottle. Celadon glaze with brush decoration of iron and cobalt, with burnished gold, height 15 cm (6 in)*

special quality to porcelain, and, indeed, the results are likely to show greater variation than the glaze effects in an oxidation firing, which are consistent and neutral.

OXIDATION FIRING

Oxidation firing is generally straightforward and needs little explanation. Porcelain can be fired fairly quickly – up to 150°C (302°F) per hour – without ill effect, although 100°C (212°F) per hour is more usual. You can soak the glaze if you wish, although you may have to reduce the temperature of the kiln slightly if the soak causes the porcelain to warp.

Soaking is useful for healing over pinholes and for bringing the glaze to a smooth finish. It also helps ensure that the temperature throughout the kiln is more even. Ten minutes can make a noticeable difference to the results, but some potters soak for much longer – between thirty minutes to an hour.

REDUCTION FIRING IN A FUEL-BURNING KILN

Reduction firing is a different process which involves the role of oxygen in the burning of a fuel such as wood, oil or gas. It must therefore be carefully supervised. Initially, the oxygen in the atmosphere is used in the burning, but, as the firing progresses, the oxygen in the kiln is used as well, and the flame has to lengthen in its attempt to find more oxygen. As the kiln increases in temperature, the flame is able to draw oxygen for burning directly from less stable oxides in

the body and glaze, thus 'reducing' them to their metal elements (or lessening the amount of oxygen present in their molecules). In this type of firing, copper and iron are changed most dramatically: copper reduces to produce lilacs, pinks and reds, and iron reduces to produce blues, greens and greys.

In reduction, the body colours of porcelain also change. Some bodies, which are quite creamy in oxidation because of the small quantity of iron oxide present, are reduced to a pale blue-grey colour as tiny amounts of red iron oxide are reduced to black iron oxide. This is a characteristic which gives the impression of the reduced porcelain being 'whiter' or 'cooler' in colour.

Reduction is normally controlled at two different places in the kiln. The first of these is the entry point of the fuel, which can involve 'forced air' powered by a mechanical blower to assist in the burning. The second is in the chimney or flue, referred to as a 'damper'. The degree of reduction is controlled by increasing or decreasing the flow of air at these two points, as well as by the amount of fuel being burned.

Most potters begin reducing at approximately 1000°C (1832°F) by adjusting any airscrews on the burners and partially closing the damper. The temperature at which you start the reduction can be varied, but this must be before the glazes melt so that the body reduces evenly (see the information on glaze faults on page 73).

As reduction takes place and the flame

lengthens in its search for oxygen, it becomes visible from the flue and spy-holes. It may be smoky and change colour – a soft yellow flame is a sign that the gases are only partially burned. However, opinions vary on the colour of the flame during reduction, possibly because the colours are different for each fuel and for the degree of reduction taking place.

During reduction, the rate at which the temperature rises will slow down. You should monitor the temperature at frequent intervals: a *drop* in temperature would signify a very heavy reduction. You must strike a balance so that the temperature continues to rise, but at a slower rate as reduction continues. Digital pyrometers are invaluable for monitoring the temperature because, unlike mechanical indicating pyrometers, they are immediately responsive even to 1 degree of temperature change.

Some potters reduce consistently from 1000°C (1832°F) up to the top temperature, and others have a brief period of oxidation at the end of the firing, coinciding with the 'soak'. If the kiln temperature fails to rise with continuous reduction, however, you will need to juggle it between oxidation and reduction by adjusting the fuel and dampers, in order to maintain a reasonable temperature rise. At the end of the firing, close the burners and the damper. You must also engage any spy-holes fully to prevent re-oxidation from air being drawn into the kiln as it cools. On some kilns, you can close the burner ports as well.

Judging the degree and quality of reduction is best done by comparing the results from several firings, although this will be a subjective decision based on your response to the colour and quality of the glaze, the body and any oxides. Although potters refer to 'over-reduction', this is difficult to quantify, and is naturally limited to some extent by the fact that over-reduction during a firing results either in a temperature drop or in a maintained temperature. The term is, however, applied to denote results that are rather dull and grey.

The nature of a flame kiln is to keep you involved with the firing and 'on your toes', whereas, with an electric kiln, a computerized controller can do it all for you. I find it hard to recall getting up very early to turn up my old kiln, now that I have a computerized controller which does everything except put in the bung! It even has a 'facility' to accommodate this problem by connecting the bung to a motor.

Even with a computerized controller or a pyrometer, however, results are subject to change: the packing of the kiln will affect the fired result, as can the condition of the elements. When firing a new kiln – whether electric or fuel-burning – for the first few times, it is better to rely on cones to monitor the temperature and check this against the controller or pyrometer. Each and every kiln *and* pyrometer have their own idiosyncrasies: 1260°C (2300°F) on one pyrometer and kiln may be 1245°C (2273°F) on another, or even 1270°C (2318°F) on a third. The main point to remember with reduction firing is that, as Peter Lane has wisely observed: 'Only experience and practice enables one fully to understand and control the firing of any particular live-flame kiln.'

REDUCTION FIRING IN AN ELECTRIC KILN

You can reduce porcelain in an electric kiln by introducing combustible material, such as wood, through the spy-hole, but – whatever the material – it obviously needs to be small enough for you to push through the hole. You must also leave space during the packing for the material to burn without touching the pots.

Most sources of information on the subject warn that the combustion of material in electric kilns quickly damages and wears the elements, but this may be dependent on the type of fuel that you use and the frequency of your reduction firings. It is quite a common practice in Japan to use a propane-gas torch to reduce in electric kilns with seemingly little detriment to the life of the elements, although these firings are spaced between biscuit firings, where no reduction takes place. (Please note that this is not a practice to be undertaken without due consideration for proper ventilation and precautions for the safe use of bottled gas.)

You can achieve the reduction of copper in an electric kiln without damage to the elements by adding silicon carbide to some glazes. This breaks down into carbon and silicon during the firing, producing a reduction micro-climate within the glaze. In his article entitled 'In the Pink', published in *Ceramic Review*, Emmanuel Cooper recommends the use of very finely ground silicon carbide (200–400 mesh) in tiny amounts of between 0.5 and 1 per cent in a fluid glaze. This is because the carbon, which is given off as a gas, causes bubbling of the surface which remains as a lava-like texture in stiffer glazes. Cooper says: 'In glazes containing a powerful flux such as calcium borate frit, or borax frit, the mixture becomes sufficiently fluid to allow the gas formed either to be released, leaving a smooth, unblemished surface, or to combine with any copper present in the glaze, changing it from its green (CuO) to its red (Cu_2O) state. Only relatively small amounts of about 0.5 per cent of copper and silicon carbide are required to achieve a strong colour ... [and] a small amount of tin oxide helps to stabilize the colour.' For reducing copper in electric kilns, he recommends the following glaze as a useful starting point.

Emmanuel Cooper: rich, deep red glaze

Soda feldspar	52
Calcium borate frit (or gerstly borate)	10
Whiting	15
China clay	5
Flint	18
Copper carbonate	0.5
Tin oxide	1
Silicon carbide (fine)	0.5

Peter Lane *Translucent porcelain bowl from 'Skies' series. Airbrushed with underglaze colours fired to 1260°C (2300°F). Diameter 26 cm (10 in)*

OTHER TYPES OF FIRING

Porcelain can be used for almost any type of firing: it has been pit-fired, sawdust-fired, saggar-fired and even, when carefully cooled, raku-fired. Apart from the possible kudos of calling a particular work 'porcelain', however, I wonder why some potters use porcelain for low-fire processes when any smooth white body would give comparable results at much less cost. In my opinion, it is only by firing porcelain to maturity that its unique qualities are realized. Two different firing methods which complement high-fired porcelain are saggar firing and soda firing.

SAGGAR-FIRED PORCELAIN

Porcelain placed in a saggar made from fire clay can be packed with charcoal or fine sawdust (and, in the case of one potter, with linseed), in order to create localized and very heavy reduction when fired to maturity in an electric or fuel-burning kiln. Where the porcelain is in direct contact with this packing material it becomes blackened, while areas which are not directly in contact with it may range through greys and whites. In reduction with charcoal, lustrous flashing can occur, which is exciting but more predictable.

Porcelain which has been burnished by compressing and smoothing the surface with a smooth pebble or a metal spoon has a fine surface which complements the smoky colour qualities of saggar firing. These are similar in colour to a sawdust firing, but have added strength because the pots can be saggar-fired to the higher temperatures of porcelain. The surface of the work, which is in contact with the charcoal or other material, should be left unglazed, but the interiors may, of course, be glazed.

SODA-FIRED PORCELAIN

Salt glazing has long been used to create the durable orange-peel surface which characterizes this firing technique. However, as the salt – which is normally introduced into a fuel-burning kiln above 1100°C (2012°F) – coats the kiln and the kiln furniture in the same way that it coats clay, the kiln can only be used for salt firing. During the salt-firing process the salt (NaCl), splits into its elements of chlorine and sodium. The sodium reacts with the surface of the clay to form a glaze, whilst the chlorine is given off as a poisonous gas. For this reason the kiln needs to be sited out of doors and away from urban areas.

Firing with soda (sodium bicarbonate) makes an acceptable alternative, as it does not break down to release chlorine but yields harmless carbon dioxide. Soda has particular advantages with porcelain, because the colours are intensified and the glaze is less like orange peel. Soda also reacts with some porcelain bodies to give orange flashing on unglazed areas.

Chris Staley soda-fires his thrown porcelain with alkaline glazes containing copper, which he partially reduces by carefully controlling the reduction in his kiln (see photograph). His glazes are dramatic: bright turquoise with flashes of red where the copper is reduced. He says: 'For me the atmosphere is critical in its effect on the finished work ... at Cone 8 (940°C [1724°F]), I try to have the lightest amount of reduction possible without oxidizing. This affects the Avery kaolin (makes it flash golden brown). Also, I believe that the lower-temperature reduction has an effect on iron- and copper-bearing glazes. I start salting when Cone 7 is down, and continue to salt at 20-minute intervals until Cone 9 is down – this usually takes $1–1\frac{1}{2}$ hours. Then I open the damper completely and let the kiln totally oxidize for 10–15 minutes. [I] then shut down the kiln and cool it slowly.'

Chris Staley: red-to-green glaze (soda firing, Cones 9–10)

Custer feldspar	50
Whiting	15
EPK China Clay	13
Dolomite	2
Flint	20
Copper carbonate	8
Iron oxide	1
Add bentonite	2

Right: **Chris Staley** Reduction soda-fired teapot. Porcelain slip with 'Rob's green glaze', height 38 cm (15 in)

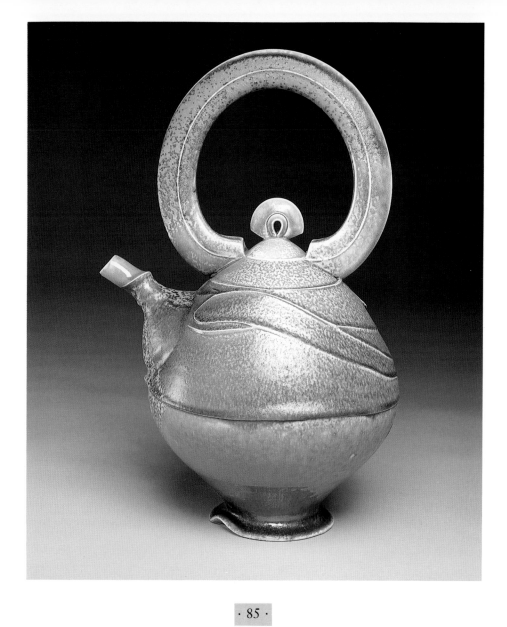

CHAPTER NINE

INDIVIDUAL APPROACHES

JOANNA HOWELLS

Joanna Howells throws and 're-assembles' her elegant and delicate porcelain tableware in a witty and imaginative way when it is leather-hard. This means that the throwing rings, instead of running horizontally, are vertical, with each side of the form revealing a spiral or part-spiral of throwing marks. She throws cups and small bowls as spheres and cuts them 'between the poles' to make two forms. Larger forms, such as teapots, are made by joining two bowls together. She partially pulls the handles, joins them to the forms, and then skilfully pulls them again to their final shape. The feet are made separately by throwing on to the leather-hard forms.

Joanna fires her porcelain in a reduction atmosphere for its qualities of whiteness and translucence, and for the clear, watery colours of the glazes.

Joanna Howells: green glaze (1270°C [2300°F] reduction)

Wood ash	30
Potash feldspar	30
Hymod at ball clay	15
Whiting	4
Silica	21
Chrome oxide	0.3

Left: **Joanna Howells** Thrown porcelain teaset. Reduction-fired

PIPPIN DRYSDALE

Brilliant colours spontaneously and exuberantly brushed on to strong, simple forms characterize Pippin Drysdale's current large-scale work in porcelain. She throws and hand-builds her generous pots to provide a surface on which she can, as she put it, 'be extravagant and experiment'.

Living in Freemantle, a busy port city in Western Australia, Pippin Drysdale is surrounded by wide open spaces – the Indian Ocean, the desert and the Australian bush – and is fascinated by their contrasts of mood, light and colour. She says that she works to 'explore the painted surface, using the environmental theme, pushing the boundaries of [my] technical and creative ability to the limit', adding that she feels the threat to the environment as a threat to herself, and that it is important for an artist to play a role in changing attitudes. 'My personal involvement with this crucial issue of the environment offers me a chance to play my role in the way

I know best, through the power of the visual medium.'

Pippin decorates most of her thrown bowls and slabbed dishes with glaze on glaze in combination with latex resist, and constantly expands her palette of coloured glazes by using them in new combinations. She applies opacified white stoneware glaze over the whole surface, and then uses latex resist to mask out areas which are to remain white. She brushes and sprays successive applications of a lower-firing glaze with added stains on top, often adding higher proportions of stain than is usual in order to keep the colours as bright as possible. This lower-fired glaze melts into and fuses with the base glaze during firing.

Pippin builds up the colours from light through to dark. The richness and range of the colours is the result of the infinite variety that can be achieved by combining them over one another, and by varying the thickness of their application.

Pippin uses latex throughout the process to mask out areas as she completes them. She sometimes uses a final application of a black glaze as a background, or to frame the drama of the freely coloured areas. The latex is peeled from the surface before firing the work. She fires the thrown pots to Orton

Left: **Pippin Drysdale** 'Logging on Parchment' (Series 90). Slabbed porcelain dish, 48 × 50 cm (19 × 20 in)

Cone 5, but often fires the slabbed dishes lower to Cone 1 in order to avoid distortion and to lessen the chance of cracking. Pippin points out that the glazes that she uses, as well as the porcelain body (which she buys ready-made), have a wide temperature range. At both temperatures the porcelain is vitrified and has a good 'ring' to it.

Pippin Drysdale: 'Jane's white glaze' (Cone 5 and higher)

Nepheline syenite	29.3
Whiting	9.7
Barium carbonate	6.4
Zinc oxide	7.9
Talc	3.9
Cresta BB ball clay	15.1
Silica 200 mesh	27.7
Zirconium silicate	14
Tin oxide	6
Bentonite	3

Pippin Drysdale: low-fired overglaze (add stains)

Ferro frit 4124	60
Ball clay	10
Whiting	20
Silica 200–300 mesh	10
Bentonite	3

EMILY MYERS

Emily Myers uses throwing and press-moulding with extrusions to make components – some of which she alters before assembling them – to create her playful 'pipe pots', or strong, simple bowl and vase forms. During this process, she says that: 'New possibilities often present themselves as I offer one form up to another.' Emily also says that she is 'continually attracted to the qualities of metal objects, particularly once they have been eroded through time. I love the patination on ancient weathered copper and metal cooking utensils, old tools, scrap car parts and manhole covers. The effect of verdigris on copper is the inspiration for my use of bright colours.'

A decorative spiral, which she makes with a wooden rib on her freely thrown pots, traces the action of her hand over the revolving form, leading the eye from the centre to the extruded rim and back again. Subtle ridges and grooves produced during the making are enhanced by the vibrant barium glazes which pool in the hollows and thin over the edges, creating tonal differences in the strong blues, turquoises and greens of the glazes.

Emily uses a wall-mounted extruder with a variety of dies to make both solid and hollow extrusions. Soft porcelain is easier to extrude, and allows her gently to curve the extrusions into shape as they emerge from the extruder. She draws an outline made with an indelible pen on the ware-board as a guide for bending extruded rims to the right shape for her press-moulded dishes. This outline has to be a little 'tighter' than the finished rim, because the soft clay extrusion will unbend slightly as it dries. She turns the extrusions frequently so that they dry evenly, and keeps them away from draughts and heat to prevent cracking and warping. (See photograph, page 38.)

With this method, the clay is handled more than usual and is prone to crack easily during the extrusion and construction of the forms, so Emily adds a minimum of 10 per cent of 30s to 80s molochite to the body. Large amounts of molochite added in this way create a torn or jagged edge on the extrusions, which she uses for its decorative effect.

Emily Myers *Thrown and extruded forms. Height 15 and 10 cm (6 and 4 in)*

Right: **Emily Myers** *Wall dish with extruded rim, 30.6 cm (12 in) diameter*

SUSAN NEMETH

The designs of Sue Nemeth's colourful and decorative bowls have been inspired by the pictures from 'over-bright' English cookbooks of the '50s and by 'the simplicity and the element of pattern in the paintings and collages of Matisse'. More recently, after a working visit to Japan, an interest in the design and presentation of Japanese food, with its appropriate style of dish and bowl, led her to take a series of photographs of the food that she had eaten. Working from these photographs, she says: 'I now take into consideration for design the shapes and colours of the dishes themselves, the food, the background, and even the shadows in the photographs. My aim is to simplify my designs through drawing from the photographs, using thick marker pens and wax crayons. The quality of the marks themselves are taken into consideration when decorating with slips and clays.'

She uses commercial body stains and oxides to colour her porcelain bodies and slips, in quantities ranging from 2–15 per cent, depending on the colour required. She builds up the decoration like a collage on a flat slab of coloured porcelain, using a combination of poured and painted slips and rolled and stained clay cut from thin sheets of coloured porcelain, which she arranges in a design and then rolls on to the base. A clean sheet of polythene prevents the colours from being smudged or transferred across the slab by the rolling pin, and she leaves the polythene in place to allow the various coloured clays to equalize in dampness.

Before pressing the decorated slab over a hump mould to form it into a bowl, Sue checks it for stiffness, and dampens it if necessary between sheets of wet newspaper. After the bowl has stiffened a little on the hump mould, she transfers it to a hollow mould to dry out further; this decreases the risk of the bowl shrinking on to the hump mould and cracking. She makes larger pieces with the addition of 80s mesh molochite in order to prevent excessive shrinkage and warping.

Sue fires the bowls in an electric kiln, packing them up to three deep in silica sand held in saggars. After biscuit firing, she sands the bowls thoroughly with wet-and-dry paper, and then sands them again after the firing to 1250°C (2282°F), to make the surface satin-smooth. She sometimes applies beeswax as a final finish.

Left: **Susan Nemeth** *Three coloured porcelain bowls, ranging in diameter from approx. 7.5 cm to 17.5 cm (3 in to 7 in)*

Above: **Susan Nemeth** *'Crab' plate. Porcelain with slips and coloured inlays, diameter 40 cm (16 in). Photograph by Tim Hill*

INKE LERCH-BRODERSEN

Inke Lerch-Brodersen decorates her carefully thrown porcelain forms with precise, geometric patterns which have subtle, changing rhythms. Inke, who shares her studio with her husband Uwe Lerch in Germany, uses porcelain because the precision and clarity of her decoration is enhanced by the whiteness and smoothness of the porcelain body. She creates the decoration using a metal needle as a sgraffito tool to scratch through coloured slips to the porcelain beneath.

Inke makes her slips very simply, using the porcelain body with additions of oxides from 5–20 per cent. She mixes and sieves these as very thin slips, which she then dries out to the right consistency on a plaster slab. She has developed her technique so that she applies the slip by spraying it on thinly after the biscuit firing, when the pots are much stronger to handle and decorate. In order for the biscuit ware to accept the slips, however, she fires the pots very low, to 850°C (1562°F), which makes them very porous.

Inke builds up her more complex patterns, where more than one coloured slip is involved, by separate applications of slip and sgrafitto, working from the darkest slip first and ending with the lightest. When the decoration is complete, she sprays the pots with glaze (sometimes applying more than one glaze), and fires them to 1260°C (2300°F).

Inke Lerch-Brodersen Porcelain bowl. *Feldspar glaze with manganese slip, 14.5 × 18.5 cm (5¾ × 7¼ in)*

Uwe Lerch and Inke Lerch-Brodersen: white opaque glaze (1260°C [2300°F])

Potash feldspar	24.7
Whiting	6.4
Zinc oxide	12.9
Barium carbonate	3.2
Talc	3.1
China clay	5.5

Inke Lerch-Brodersen
Porcelain bowl, decorated
with coloured slips,
height 15 cm (6 in)

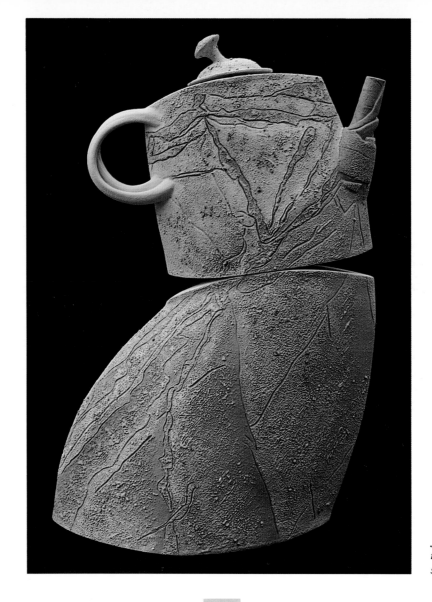

Jenny Beavan *'Rock Formation in Thin Section'. Teapot with stand, height 45 cm (18 in)*

JENNY BEAVAN

The success and integrity of Jenny Beavan's vessel forms rely not only on her considerable technical skill in using slabbed, thrown and coiled elements, and on her sense of colour, texture and place, but also on her ability to combine all these elements in an exciting and satisfying way. She says that she 'seeks to synthesize expression, form and function'.

Jenny uses porcelain to make her brightly coloured and textured vessels, with their dry, undulating surfaces, because of its plastic qualities in the making. She also likes its whiteness, durability and density when fired, as these characteristics enhance the tones and colours of the slips that she uses to 'illustrate' the surfaces of her work.

Jenny bases each piece on a vessel form, and makes them largely using slabs, which she rolls by hand and incises before draping them over curved formers. Once the decorated slabs have stiffened, they are trimmed carefully. She then joins them with a mitred edge where necessary, and reinforces the join with a thin, soft coil of porcelain, which is smoothed on the inside.

She supports forms with curved bases on a thick layer of sponge, and, before finally closing the form at the top, carefully strokes and pushes the walls from the inside to articulate the exterior surfaces. Lids, and any interlocking parts, are thrown and turned, and cut to form oval shapes before joining them to the main body of the vessel. She pulls her handles, and forms spouts round a wooden dowel.

She applies strongly coloured slips to the surface, with the addition of beach sand, decomposed granite and found raw materials which texture the surface richly. She glazes the interiors of the vessels with a transparent glaze, while leaving the exteriors largely unglazed, although she sometimes uses a very thin application of glaze to help the sand to bond onto the surface of the work.

Jenny Beavan's brightly coloured and textured vessels, with their dry, gently undulating surfaces and incised lines, are an amalgam of the stimulus of the Cornish landscape around her and her response to it: 'I draw my stimulus from my immediate environment: the coastline and landforms of Cornwall, with its wealth of mineral deposits. I am struck by the relationship of the images displayed in the surface landforms, the geological structure underlying these landforms and their component minerals as they are seen in microscopic-thin section, to the extent that I am feeling moved towards an examination in my work of the material fabric of the Earth and its relationship to the constituents of the Universe. I see the work as an amalgamation of form-making and image-making, in which all component materials are of equal importance. The finished pieces represent a minor interruption in a process of disintegration and movement, rather like a recording of time and matter.'

MASAMICHI YOSHIKAWA

Masamichi Yoshikawa's work has been exhibited in his native Japan and around the world in Europe, the USA and Russia. In addition to his personal studio he has more recently set up a workshop in Tokoname, Japan. His porcelain comes from Amakusa in Kyusyu, southern Japan – the same source of the porcelain that was used in Old Imari and Arita ware. He says: 'the ingredients are simple and natural, but I visit the professional clay-makers each year to have the clay adjusted to my needs'.

Masamichi reduction-fires to 1300°C (2372°F) in a gas kiln. He makes many of his slabbed forms from clay of varying thicknesses, which he shapes by scraping and carving with a selection of knives. He joins the carved slabs using porcelain slip and scoring. He is particularly careful to dry the work slowly and carefully over a long period of time.

Masamichi always pays very careful attention to biscuit firing, heating the kiln extremely slowly up to 300°C (572°F). His thickest pieces take up to 72 hours for a biscuit firing, although he adds: 'I am interested in warping and distortion. I like to use it as an expression. Previously I was interested in the precise, cool feeling of porcelain, but now my feeling has changed to sensuousness.'

He comments on the role of the artist in Japanese society, saying that 'while working within the traditional framework of Chun-glazed, reduction-fired porcelain, I have taken the traditional materials and techniques of porcelain to create a synthesis that not only reflects the tradition and culture from which it comes, but also speaks to us of contemporary forms and feelings.'

Masamichi Yoshikawa 'Orebes Changed to Blue and White'. Slabbed porcelain dish, 25 × 25 × 42 cm (10 × 10 × 16½ in)

RUSSELL COATES

Russell Coates learned the traditional techniques and aesthetics of enamelling on porcelain in Japan, and continues to mix his own enamels and underglaze blue from recipes passed down through generations of Kutani potters. The strong, transparent enamel colours have a jewel-like quality and depth when painted over the underglaze blue, and are enhanced by the faintly blue-grey colour of the reduced porcelain background. There are five traditional enamel colours: green and purple (which tend to predominate in the designs), and yellow, red and blue. Combinations of yellow and green are also popular as dominant colours, whereas combinations of yellow and purple, or yellow and blue in large areas, are not thought as pleasing and are rarely found.

These enamels basically consist of one tone, and so one of Russell's problems in working with them lies in producing an illusion of space in the design, and achieving a 'shaded' effect. He overcomes this largely by using a framework of underglaze blue beneath the glaze, and by adding some extra-fine detail and pattern, which he paints in black (using calcined manganese), on top of the glaze but beneath the enamels. These various layers of decoration create a mysterious and subtle quality which draws you into intimate contact with the work, while, from a distance, the carefully juxtaposed and tiny areas of colour seem to blend together, creating an illusion of more than five colours.

Russell has to plan his designs carefully before glazing, and drawing and sketching form an essential link between his ideas and the finished work. He often draws the designs for the underglaze blue directly on to the biscuit porcelain using a pencil (which burns out during the firing), and then paints it. Russell also uses fine tissue paper – a Japanese technique – to transfer complex tracings from drawings on paper to the surface of both biscuit and glazed pots. He makes the tracing on the tissue using a biro, and then carefully 'paints' the reverse side of the tissue with finely ground charcoal. When he presses this tissue over the pot, a light outline of charcoal is left as a guide for the decoration. This can be used either for the underglaze blue on the biscuit, or for the black manganese under enamel painting, which he applies to the fired glaze.

Russell mixes his own underglaze blue, using a combination of five or more oxides finely ground with calcined China clay. He formulates the mixture carefully to create just the right shade and hue of blue when the pot is reduction-fired, and mixes this with green tea as a medium before painting it on to the biscuit porcelain. He dampens the biscuit first with water to reduce the porosity and to prevent the brushstrokes from dragging on the surface.

For successful enamel painting, the glazed surfaces of the pots must be de-greased before the enamels are applied. Russell uses a cotton swab soaked in gelatine to wipe over the surfaces. This leaves a thin matt coating, holding the enamel and the black manganese underpainting on the glaze before it is fired. He mixes up the gelatine in small quantities, as, being a natural product, it deteriorates quickly. He dissolves it in water and boils it until a thin layer painted on the hands sticks them together, and then it is ready to use.

Russell's earlier work was directly influenced by both his Japanese experiences, where he learned Japanese ceramic traditions and the cultural influences of architecture, garden design and landscape, and by his interest in abstract art. Gradually, new themes evolved as he moved from London to the rural setting of a small Somerset town in south-west England.

Many of his designs now have pictorial images of birds and fish within landscapes, which are juxtaposed with decorative centrepieces, or borders. The design roots of this new decoration can be traced to European traditions, to Saxon and Celtic patterns, to carpets and tapestries, and to the stained-glass 'rose' windows of the great European cathedrals. His techniques of producing the startlingly complex patterns of the enamels over blue-and-white painted porcelain may owe their origins to Japan, but Russell's designs are a synthesis of skill and the development of a personal style that reflects his English roots as well as his experience in Japan. A full description of

Russell Coates's techniques can be found in John Gibson's book *Pottery Decoration* (see the Bibliography on page 109).

Russell Coates: underglaze blue (for reduction firing: 1280°C [2300°F])

Cobalt blue	20
Manganese dioxide	22
Nickel oxide	5
Copper oxide	5
Iron oxide	6
Calcined China clay	50

Calcine this mixture in a biscuit-porcelain dish at 1100°C (2012°F) for two hours, chip out the cindered mass and grind it to a fine powder. This blue is for reduction firing, and is black when fired in oxidation.

Russell Coates *Dish with Celtic cross and fish border*

CHAPTER TEN

WHY USE PORCELAIN?

Riddle me re, riddle me re
What rings like a bell, but pours out tea?
What is stronger than bone and smoother
than silk,
Made from earth, but the colour of milk?
– Yet through it you can see.

The qualities of porcelain, which attract the maker to its use and the buyer to its purchase, are very wide-ranging – so much so that what inspires and pleases some will be of secondary or little importance to others. The potter Peter Lane, who has written and lectured extensively on the subject of porcelain, says: 'It is a delightful medium, which allows one to be precise in the execution of form and surface treatment to a degree not possible in other clay bodies. It has that marvellous quality of translucency and delicacy when potted thinly enough and with sensitivity. It is also white, so colour need not be sullied by iron or other impurities.'

Derek Clarkson, who is known for his finely carved and decorated porcelain, adds: '[Porcelain] has a wonderfully distinctive ring when struck … the gently fluxing nature of the body with feldspathic glazes at high temperatures, when fired in a reducing atmosphere, lends a seductive quality.' Yet Russell Coates, who studied on-glaze enamel techniques in Japan, comments: 'I never aim to get porcelain translucent; a lot of oriental porcelain is quite heavy with no intention to make it translucent, but it is almost *the* quality in the West. A lot of Imari [an area in Japan, and also the name given to the renowned enamelled porcelain made there] is quite chunky but with rich, brilliant colours.'

The different working qualities of individual bodies also inspire makers to use porcelain, but David Leach wisely points out: 'Maybe we call it all "porcelain", but really it is like referring to bodies as "stoneware"; there are many different qualities [of porcelain], and the different nuances should be taken into account. You must find one that suits you.'

Porcelain as a material can be unforgiving and demanding, and attracts a certain kind of potter to work with it. As David Leach comments: 'It is the particular kind of person one is – you can't imagine Michael Cardew, for instance, having the meticulous patience that porcelain most needs. So you need to be a person who is prepared to work slowly and very carefully and rather meticulously – at the opposite end of the scale, as it were, to the people who are very robust, spontaneous, and do things quickly and can't be bothered with detail. You do get contradictions to that, exceptions to the rule: there are potters who aren't so concerned with the delicacy end of it. Translucence doesn't interest them … spontaneous people want to keep the thing very vigorous and very alive; want to work quickly and not too delicately because they are afraid that, if they do, in their view, they will kill the life in it.'

Colin Pearson is a potter who uses porcelain more 'spontaneously', but, as he says: 'I prefer stoneware to use, but I like the

Margaret O'Rorke *Thrown, cut and re-assembled porcelain light. Height 24 cm (9½in)*

finished [porcelain] product, so I use it, although it is against my normal temperament ... I accept it as a challenge. It is difficult! I like the effects of colour and translucency that I can get. I suppose because I do [make] stoneware I like the contrast – the other side of the coin from the more refined porcelain.'

QUALITIES, LIMITATIONS AND PARADOX

When you examine the qualities and limitations of porcelain, you can begin to see that some characteristics can be viewed from either perspective. For example, what could be regarded as a limitation might become a useful quality when exploited in a particular way, and herein lie some of the paradoxes of porcelain. As a clay, porcelain is extremely smooth and fine to work, and may also – depending on the body – be anything from extremely plastic to handle to very short. Russell Coates describes it very succinctly as 'smooth and tricky'!

Porcelain has a reputation among potters and the public for its fineness, thinness and apparent fragility, but fired porcelain is in fact stronger than any other clay, even when it is on a small scale or thin. This is an

Derek Emms Lidded porcelain pot. Engraving under blue-green celadon, height 38 cm (15 in)

advantage for ceramic jewellery, which, when it is not made of porcelain, is often chunky but easily broken. Porcelain can also be robustly worked and generously thick (as in Masamichi Yoshikawa's work: see pages 34 and 98); then it has a strange, iceberg-like depth and coolness.

Whether porcelain is thin or thickly formed, when glazed with a transparent or a milky glaze, it has a particularly subtle and magical quality, where that which is 'solid and strong' can seemingly be pierced by the notion that you can see into it. This notion is less imaginary when the porcelain is thin and mature enough to become translucent. If you hold it to the light, the shape of your fingers will be clearly outlined through the material; one is reminded of the power of X-rays revealing the bones, or possibly a metaphysical metaphor for locating, within the body, the presence of the spirit or soul. Translucence seems particularly appropriate on small bowls or cups, or for lights (see Margaret O'Rorke's work on page 102), but is more difficult to achieve over the whole of a large piece, and can appear inappropriately sharp and brittle.

Porcelain has a tendency to slump from too much wetting, but, perversely, it also dries out suddenly. These can be useful characteristics which allow the manipulation and deformation of the form, even when it is fairly hard. The tendency of porcelain to warp and slump can continue in the firing, however, either ruining a carefully considered

form, or imbuing other work with a sense of movement and energy.

Porcelain is admired for its whiteness. Indeed, the *quality of whiteness* forms a whole aesthetic on its own, especially in Japan, where particular pottery dynasties such as Kakiemon and Imaemon are revered for the quality and vibrance of their onglaze decoration, and also for the *particular quality* of whiteness of their porcelain bodies. Working with the whiteness of porcelain and a transparent or single-coloured glaze, the maker can explicitly draw attention to the subtlety and precision of form, whereas those who work with decoration use the whiteness of the porcelain to show the freshness and depth of colours, sometimes at the expense of the form.

Unglazed, high-fired porcelain is a beautiful material on its own – smooth and sensuous to touch, but with a density more akin to the coolness and hardness of stone than the qualities of warmth and earthiness usually associated with clay. When stained with colour and inlaid or marbled, however, unglazed porcelain has a quality particular to itself, being smooth and durable like stone but having the potential for bright, vibrant colours generally associated with more contemporary materials, such as resins and plastics. Stained porcelain has the potential for such fine detail that it belies the human hand, and has a surface with great integrity.

Dorothy Feibleman observes that 'for carvability [when leather-hard], porcelain

allows [for] precision, without being a rigid material like metal or wood'. However, the alchemy of fire changes the porcelain, which was once able to be worked back and forth between plasticity and hardness, so that it becomes infinitely more durable than wood or metal.

INSPIRATION AND DEVELOPMENT

It is true that porcelain must be more thoroughly prepared and carefully handled, more evenly and slowly dried, more carefully packed and fired, and requires more attention to form and finish than any other clay. It is not enough simply to gain technical mastery over the material, however, for this is not the only source of the artist's power. Ideas and inspiration are as important as technique. The development of ideas is fed by a continuum of intimate contact with tools, materials and fire, and is inspired by the emergence of a personal visual language. As Gordon Cooke remarks: 'one is constantly digesting stimuli', whether direct or indirect. Visual language is formed and informed by our experience, which requires careful 'editing' and sorting to make personal sense.

The development of a personal language can be achieved in many ways. The activities of drawing and painting enable you to *select* what interests *you*, and, in putting this on paper, you are already re-making and

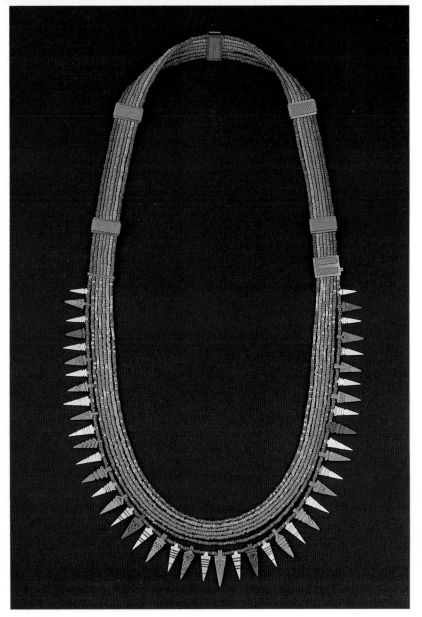

Dorothy Feibleman *Parian porcelain necklace with 18-carat gold. Laminated and marbled. (Collection of Mark and Carmen Holman)* Photograph by Thomas Ward, courtesy of Bonhams

transposing the image or idea as your own. In my opinion, drawing is the only activity which will enable you to sustain the 'looking' process for long periods of time (with the possible exception of meditation), particularly when what you are looking at is static. Photography, used selectively, provides another useful tool for recording stimuli, for marking things out as 'particular', or for isolating detail. The photograph is capable of catching and freezing the most fleeting of moments, enabling you to examine and re-examine a sensation, or a moment in time, at will.

You can also feed your inspiration by the objects that you collect about you. What drew you to them? What is the quality you enjoy about a particular object? The smoothness of a beach-washed pebble? The torn and faded quality of a fragment from an old poster? The bright, cheerful brashness of a cheap plastic toy?

Ideas and inspiration do need to be tempered by critical awareness, however, and – although the view of criticism can be a negative one – it may be helpful to think of critical awareness as a form of internal dialogue. This conversation entails comparison, for example: 'this works better than that because . . .', and logic, such as: 'what are the steps and processes that I need to work through?', but is also a way of breaking the rules and accepted methods of working, so that you might think: 'what if I do it this way?'

Gordon Cooke *Slabbed porcelain pot. Oxides and stains were painted on the raw slab, allowed to dry, scored with blades and then rolled again. Height 27 cm (10¾ in)*

When the work is flowing well, it is either because the maker is at one with the process of making, or is energized and inspired by the potential of what could be done – by the internal dialogue of: 'what if I . . .?' – when the next step or development comes to mind and the work progresses.

THE FUTURE

It does not require deep insight to predict that pollution and the consumption of finite resources will affect the techniques that we deploy as potters. We must understand the dangers of pollution – possibly more so than other craft workers – because many of the materials and some of the processes that we use are toxic to a greater or lesser degree. They are capable of damaging the health of the potter and, indirectly, of polluting the water supply, the atmosphere or the earth.

WASTE DISPOSAL
Some countries already have legislation in place to regulate the safe use and disposal of particular materials. Although these regulations often only apply to large organizations, this is no reason for studio potters to be complacent. There are two main areas of concern: raw materials (in particular, glazes and ceramic colours, which may be toxic), and firing procedures (which should proceed with an efficient and clean use of energy). The level of general awareness about the safe use of ceramic glazes and colours has

improved considerably over the last two decades, with information and advice available from pottery suppliers and, in Great Britain and the USA, through literature from government agencies and independent publications.

Although potters are increasingly aware of the safe handling of materials in use, it is surprising how thoughtlessly toxic materials are discarded, simply by washing them away. A clay trap should be compulsory beneath a sink to catch this waste and, more importantly, it must be *regularly emptied* and the slurry dried out and carefully disposed of. (Many local authorities have specific provisions and regulations concerning the disposal of harmful waste.)

It is, of course, even better to prevent the residues of ceramic colours entering the water system at all. By partially drying out palettes and water pots and mopping up the residue with damp newspaper, you can discard them more safely in the rubbish collection. This is particularly important in urban areas, where the water is frequently recycled through the system.

ENERGY SAVING

The maturing temperature of some porcelain bodies has been gradually reduced from 1300°C (2372°F) to approximately 1260°C (2300°F) or lower, making a saving in both cost and energy. A number of contemporary potters have experimented to reduce the firing temperature of porcelain even lower, to around Cone 6, by using different fluxes to alter the maturing temperature of the body and glaze, while retaining some translucence. However, the substitution of materials to lower the maturing temperature of porcelain bodies can also change the handling qualities of the clay and its behaviour in the kiln, and the maturing temperature becomes critical; even a slight over-firing can cause sudden deformation.

It would seem that the particular qualities of fired porcelain associated with soft-sheened, unctuous glazes and reasonable handling qualities are more easily achieved with the higher temperatures, so it is important that kilns are as efficient as possible. This has been made realistic since the widespread use of ceramic fibre and its associated materials, such as board and paper. These newer materials are used for modern kilns, but older kilns can also be insulated with these materials. Information about their safe use and attachment is available from all leading ceramic-fibre suppliers.

THE POTENTIAL OF PORCELAIN

The last two decades have seen a tremendous increase in the popularity of porcelain, and in the scope of its expression. There are more and more instances where the distinctions between what might be termed 'industrial' and 'handmade', as well as 'art' and 'craft', are blurred. The potential of clay as a means of expression, as well as (or in spite of) its functional role, is described, along with other crafts, in *The Eloquent Object* (see the Bibliography on page 109):

'"Modern craft" in the USA is the aesthetic paradox of a post-industrial culture. The very technology that almost eliminated the crafts maker from the culture has freed him to expand his creative scope. Once the useful machine-made product became accessible to everyone, cheaper than you could make at home, craft was no longer required to be useful. Craft is the expression of the culture's resistance to the depersonalizing forces of technological and corporate power.'

The two comments below show some of the contemporary preoccupations and attractions of using porcelain as a means of expression and, inadvertently, hint at the enduring but paradoxical qualities of all great pots – that they are 'timeless' yet 'of their time'.

Delan Cookson (pages 16 and 70) says: 'As a ceramic artist, I am not really interested in making useful, functional pots or in re-creating some mythical past. I would like my pots to be very much of today. My objective is to play on the association of ideas through using forms which have some resemblance to something we all think we recognize and thus hopefully will find intriguing or even stimulating. These present pieces have an anthropomorphic origin. The attraction of throwing is that it forces you to simplify everything and concentrate on the essence of the idea, a bit like poetry.'

Geoffrey Eastop, writing in *Ceramic Review* in October 1980, explains: 'I have become aware of the need to try and discover my own capacity for originality, independently of temporary fashion. The relationship between the practical means by which the work is carried out and the character of the final result retains a permanent magnetic effect; one keeps coming back for more.'

Paula Winokur '*Mantel for Three Bowls*'. *Constructed and assembled porcelain slabs, with thrown bowls. 142 × 127 × 30.5 cm (56 × 50 × 12 in).* Photograph copyright Eric Mitchell

BIBLIOGRAPHY

AXEL, Jan and McCREADY, K., *Porcelain: Traditions and New Visions* (Watson-Guptill)

AYRES, John, IMPEY, Oliver and MALLET, J.V.G., *Porcelain for Palaces* (Oriental Ceramic Society)

BEITTEL, Kenneth R., *Zen and the Art of Pottery* (Weatherhill)

BLACKMAN, Audrey, *Rolled Pottery Figures* (Pitman)

CLINTON, Margery, *The Complete Potter: Lustres* (B.T. Batsford)

COOPER, Emmanuel, *A History of World Pottery* (B.T. Batsford)

COOPER, Emmanuel, *Cooper's Book of Glaze Recipes* (B.T. Batsford)

COOPER, Emmanuel, *The Complete Potter: Glazes* (B.T. Batsford)

COOPER, Emmanuel and ROYLE, Derek, *Glazes for the Studio Potter* (B.T. Batsford)

CURRIE, Ian, *Stoneware Glazes: A Systematic Approach* (Bootstrap Publishers)

FOURNIER, Robert, *An Illustrated Dictionary of Practical Pottery*

FRASER, Harry, *Ceramic Faults and their Remedies* (A & C Black)

FRENCH, Neil, *Industrial Ceramics* (Oxford University Press)

FRITH, Donald, *Mould Making for Ceramics* (A & C Black)

GIBSON, John, *Pottery Decoration* (A & C Black)

HAMER, Frank and Jane, *Clays* (Pitman)

HAMILTON, David, *A Thames and Hudson Manual of Pottery and Ceramics* (Thames and Hudson)

HOPPER, Robin, *The Ceramic Spectrum* (HarperCollins)

LANE, Peter, *Studio Porcelain* (Pitman)

LEACH, Bernard, *A Potter's Book* (Faber & Faber)

LEACH, Bernard, *A Potter in Japan, 1952–1954* (Faber & Faber)

MEDLEY, Margaret, *The Chinese Potter* (Phaidon)

PHILBROOK MUSEUM OF ART (USA), *The Eloquent Object* (distributed by University of Washington Press, Seattle)

PHILLIPS, Anthony, *The Complete Potter: Slips and Slipware* (B.T. Batsford)

RAWSON, Phillip and LEGEZA, Laszlo, *Tao, The Chinese Philosophy of Time and Change* (Thames and Hudson)

RHODES, Daniel, *Stoneware and Porcelain* (Pitman)

ROGERS, Mary, *On Pottery and Porcelain* (Alpha Books)

SANDEMAN, Alison, *Working with Porcelain* (Pitman)

SANDERS, Herbert H., *The World of Japanese Ceramics* (Kodansha)

SIMPSON, Penny, KITTO, Lucy and SODEOKA, Kanji, *The Japanese Pottery Handbook* (Kodansha)

SOUTHWELL, Sheila, *Painting China and Porcelain* (Blandford)

WILLIAMS, Nigel, *Porcelain Repair and Restoration* (British Museum Publications)

WOOD, Nigel, *Oriental Glazes* (Pitman)

LIST OF SUPPLIERS

UK

Acme Marls Ltd
Bournes Bauk
Burslem
Stoke-on-Trent ST2 3DW

WG Ball Ltd
Longton Mill, Anchor Road
Longton
Stoke-on-Trent

Bath Potters Supplies
2 Dorset Close
Bath BA2 3RF

Briar Wheels and Supplies Ltd
Whitsbury Road
Fordingbridge
Hants SP6 1NQ

Ceramatech
Units 16–17
Frontier Works
33 Queen Street
London N17 8JA

Cromartie Kilns Ltd
Park Hall Road
Longton
Stoke-on-Trent ST3 5AY

Clayman
251b Pagham Road
Nyetimber
Bognor Regis
W. Sussex PO21 3QB

WJ Doble
Newdown Sand and Clay Pits
St Agnes
Cornwall

Dragon Ceramex
5 Norris Park
Congresbury
Avon BS19 5HB

English China Clays Ltd
John Keay House
St Austell
Cornwall PL25 4DJ

Essex Kilns Ltd
Woodrolf Road
Tollesbury
Malden
Essex CM9 8SJ

Ferro Great Britain
Wombourne
Wolverhampton WV5 8DA

Gladstone Engineering Co. Ltd
Foxley Lane
Milton
Stoke-on-Trent ST2 7EH

Kilns and Furnaces Ltd
Keele Street
Tunstall
Stoke-on-Trent ST6 5AS

Laser Kilns Ltd
Unit 9
Crispin Industrial Centre
Angel Road Works
London N18 2DT

Pilling Pottery
School Lane
Pilling
Nr Garstang
Lancs PR3 6HB

Potclays Ltd
Brickkiln Lane
Etruria
Stoke-on-Trent
ST4 7BP

Potters Mate
Cust Hall
Toppesfield
Halstead
Essex

Potterycrafts Ltd
Campbell Road
Stoke-on-Trent ST4 4ET

also at:
2 Norbury Trading Estate
Craignish Avenue
London SW16 4RW

Reward-Clayglaze Ltd
Units A and B
Brookshouse Industrial Estate
Cheadle
Stoke-on-Trent ST10 1PW

also at:
Kings Yard Pottery
Talbot Road
Rickmansworth
Herts WD3 1HW

and
8–10 Ingate Place
London SW8 3NS

Spencroft Ceramics Ltd
Spencroft Road
Holditch Industrial Estate
Newcastle
Staffs ST5 7BP

Stanton Pottery Supplies
Canal Lane, Westport Lake
Tunstall
Stoke-on-Trent ST6 4NZ

Valentine Clay Products
The Sliphouse
Birches Head Road
Hanley
Stoke-on-Trent ST1 6LH
(for 'Audrey Blackman'
porcelain)

USA

Amaco American Art Clay Co.
4717 West Sixteenth Street
Indianapolis
Indiana 46222

ART Studio Clay Co.
1555 Louis Avenue
Elkgrove
IL 60007

Cedar Heights Clay Co.
50 Portsmouth Road
Oak Hill
Ohio

Ceramic Supply of New York
and New Jersey
7 Route 46 West
Lodi NJ 07644

Continental Clay Co.
1101 Stenson Blvd NE
Minneapolis
Min 55413

Del-Val Potters Supply Co.
7600 Queen Street
Wyndmoor PA 19118

Ferro Corporation
PO Box 6650
Cleveland
Ohio 44101

Mason Colour and Chemical
PO Box 76
E. Liverpool
Ohio 43920

Pemco Products Group
5601 Eastern Avenue
Baltimore
Maryland 21224

Randall Pottery Inc.
Box 774
Alfred
New York 14802

AUSTRALIA

Ceramic Supply Co.
61 Lakemba Street
Belmore
NSW 2192

Diamond Ceramic Supplies Ltd
50–52 Geddes Street
Mulgrave
Melbourne
Victoria 3170

Walker Ceramics
Boronia Road
Wantirna
Victoria
PO Box 208
Bayswater 3153

INDEX